Dr. Theodore L. Dones

SEEDS OF DEFILEMENT

MESSENGERS OF FIRE MINISTRIES

Note: In order to show no acknowledgment for satan, every reference to him will reflect a lowercase "s" regardless of this breaking the rules of grammar.

Dear Readers,

If you have enjoyed this book, I would like to ask you to prayerfully consider leaving an honest review on Amazon.com (https://www.amazon.com), or email it to me so that I can place it on my website.

Thank you!

CONTACT US

Speaking Engagements, Conferences, Crusades & Seminars

Email Us: teddones@messengersoffire.org

MESSENGERS OF FIRE MINISTRIES

WWW.FACEBOOK.COM/MESSENGERSOFFIREMINISTRIES

WWW.TWITTER.COM/APOSTLETEDDONES

WWW.MESSENGERSOFFIRE.ORG

CONTENTS

DEDICATION

First and foremost, I want to dedicate this book to the Lord Jesus Christ. Secondly, I would also like to dedicate this book to my beautiful wife, Janet, who has stood beside me through thick and thin. I am grateful for all her many hours of prayer and intercession for me as I labored in the word for many days and weeks; so, this message from the Lord could be clearly presented to the people of God. I believe with this message they will be delivered from the bondage of satan.

I would also like to thank my precious daughter who gave up years of being with her parents as we travelled across the United States so that we could help bring liberty and freedom to God's people in Jesus name!

Dr. Theodore Dones

Mondo De La Vega Foreword

Every artist, sculptor, boat builder or creator of anything cannot help but leave some part of themselves behind in their creation. God did the same with each of us when he created the world and everything in it. Seeds of Defilement refers to the seed that God planted into each and every one of us at the time of creation, his breath of life.

God created by speaking it into existence (Genesis 1:3). Words are very powerful things. But with every spoken word there is a thought that comes first. Where do your thoughts come from? Are they from God? How can you know? The only way to know God's voice in your life is to know his written word. Do your thoughts agree with what is written in the Bible?

When Jesus was tempted after his forty days in the wilderness he was hungry and the tempter told him to turn the stones into bread. How did Jesus respond? Matthew 4:4 (NIV) says that Jesus responded by quoting scripture; "It is written: Man shall not live on bread alone, but on every word that comes from the mouth of God." With every temptation Jesus quoted scripture as his response.

Dr. Theodore Dones has written a book that will help all of us in our struggle to live our lives for God's purpose and not our own. He will guide you step-by-step down the path using scripture as his reference, giving you his unique insight into God's word.

Mondo De La Vega

Co-Host of The Jim Bakker Show

FORWARD BY APOSTOLIC REVIVALIST WARREN HUNTER

As I read through this Book, Mark 4:24 jumped out at me, "Then He said to them, "Take heed what you hear. With the same measure you use, it will be measured to you; and to you who hear, more will be given." Mark 4:24

Dr. Theodore Dones takes great time and accuracy to make sure that the individual receives the pure seed of the Word at the same time developing within the reader the ability to see what is an impure word contaminated buy false ideas and doctrines that keep individuals from coming into the fullness of Christ, Be blessed reading.

Apostolic Revivalist

Warren Hunter

SWORD MINISTRIES INTERNATIONAL

ENDORSEMENT

There is a television show on TBN starring Mike Rowe called, 'Somebody's gotta do it." The intro to that program uses these words: 'My name is Mike Rowe and I am on a mission looking for someone on a mission." Great intro! Dr. Ted Dones is a man on a mission! He is a follower of Jesus Christ who takes his relationship with the Lord very seriously! There is no middle ground or gray area for this man on a mission. I like the fact that he is a man of God on a mission for God and that his faith is paramount in all he does. When you hear him preach or read one of his books, you will quickly learn that his profession of faith in Jesus is not wishy washy nor ambivalent about Jesus. As you read this book, you will quickly realize just how serious Dr. Dones approaches faith, understanding the Word of God and application of those great truths contained in the Bible. You will get to know him through the written words on these pages and you will be blessed. The consideration of the Word of God being a seed that the Holy Spirit wants to plant in your heart will challenge you; charge you; and change you to become more faithful and filled with hope. Then you too, will be on a mission for Jesus! I am so delighted to call him a friend; a brother in Christ; and a fellow servant who is with me on a mission!

Dr. G.L. French

Life Renewed Ministries

Buckner, Kentucky

ENDORSEMENT

Many are the teachings of man, but the truth is only found in the revelation of God's word. Jesus, rebuking the Pharisees said, "You teach the doctrine of man, and ignore the commandments of God." What I do love about my dear friend Dr. Theodore Dones, is that he never compromises the truth of God's word, regardless of the consequences.

The Lord confirms His word with miracles, signs, and wonders. Miracles, signs and wonders are the children's bread, and the Lord is using Dr. Dones as He used the apostles in the book of Acts. The church is in desperate need of the truth that sets the captives free. It is a commandment from Jesus Christ to raise the dead, and to heal all manner of sickness and diseases and Dr. Dones is being obedient to God's word as the Lord uses him.

My encouragement to every believer is to please read this book, and the Lord will give you good insight into the truth of His promises for you."

God bless you,

Pastor Joseph Reyes

Jesus Christ Unlimited Ministries

ENDORSEMENT

Apostles are wise master builders. Jesus Christ first gave to His church, Apostles. Without them the church would be abused by every wind of doctrine. The ability to identify abusive doctrine is an Apostolic grace.

Scripture teaches that we should not sow our field with two types of seed, because whatever a man sows, that he will reap.

In this book Apostle, Dr. Theodore Dones clearly reveals the two types of seed in the earth. This study will show you a wise master builder at work. This writing will equip you with revelation to deal with "Seeds of Defilement".

I know the deep love Apostle, Dr. Theodore Dones has for the Church and from this love comes Godly wisdom, with both academic and revelatory strategy from Scripture to deliver to the reader who reads this book.

"In all your getting, get understanding", this book will help you do exactly that.

Apostle Ricardo Watson, Ph.D.

Lion of Zion

ENDORSEMENT

Dr Theodore Dones is called of God for such a time as this to bring the Body of Christ into Godly alignment through the power of the Holy Spirit. It is with great honor that I endorse this book "Seeds of Defilement". This is not just another book to read but a life changing investment to you and your generation.

This generation is giving something and that is the truth that has to be spoken. As you begin to read this book you will not want to stop until the end. There is an abundance of truth in it, because it will bring clarity to the things you may be facing at this present moment.

Dr. Theodore Dones is led by the Spirit of God to deal with the deep things that will liberate us as a people. As you read this book, your life will never be the same ever again. This book is long overdue and is highly recommended.

In Christ Service.

Gary Simons; Cape Town, South Africa

INTRODUCTION

"And God said, let the earth bring forth grass, the herb yielding seed, and the fruit tree yielding fruit after his kind, whose seed is in itself, upon the earth: and it was so."

Genesis 1:11 KJV

Maybe you remember visiting a game reserve for hunting or sight-seeing. What about a trip to the forest for picnic or hike? Perhaps you enjoy nurturing a small garden in a courtyard, tending to specific flowers and watering certain trees? These are all amazing experiences, that reflect the beauty of nature and define relaxing hobbies for some. I personally think trees, as the wind blows through them creating whistling, jostling and whimpering sounds, are beautiful, spectacular natural creations.

Truly, the existence of trees, whatever various kinds are not magical or spontaneous, in and of themselves, per se. Everything you see today; river, flowers, birds, caves, canyons, animals, even humans, originated from a source, which in most cases tends to seem very small and insignificant in the beginning stages, but later becomes too conspicuous to remain unnoticed.

Even a tree has a source and this source is its seed. A seed is sown or planted before you ever find or see a tree. However, wherever you plant your seed, it is bound to grow in the exact location it was intended and or planted.

For example, no one plants an orange seed in the north and expects to have an orange tree spring forth far south. A wise planter carefully chooses his soil, his seed and his season.

It is by law of nature that you shall harvest from the seed of which you planted. You may ask, what do I mean? Simply put, no one plants a seed and reaps something different from the seed planted. As this would imply that you cannot plant an apple seed and expect to have a coconut tree? Every seed produces its own tree with its destined fruit bearing seed of the same.

The Seed

Let's look at this a little deeper. A seed is a tiny grain which reproduces and becomes a mature tree bearing fruit, when sown in soil. A seed producing a tree which then forms fruit that contains seeds of the same. Hence, a seed has the potential of replicating itself when planted.

I implore you to consider that seeds are not sown on soil alone but can also be sown in the human heart. How? You may ask. It is simply by the things we *see* and *hear.* I am simply implying that words and images are "seeds". Whatever we hear and see is absorbed into the soil of our hearts and begins to reproduce and form us.

The Bible says;

"Thou shalt not sow thy vineyard with divers seeds: lest the fruit of thy seed which thou hast sown, and the fruit of thy vineyard, be defiled."

Deuteronomy 22:9 KJV

When God speaks, His words become seeds upon our hearts. It is your responsibility to either nurture the seed of the Word of God so that it can become a great tree. Or you can allow the life bearing qualities of the seed to be choked to death by external defilement.

The War against the Seed

You see the devil targets the seed of God's Word in our hearts in an attempt to corrupt it, by introducing a counterfeit fruit bearing a different "seed" of sorts. The Bible says:

"But while men slept, his enemy came and sowed tares among the wheat, and went his way."

Matthew 13:25 KJV

The devil understands the principles of sowing seeds, he knows that he doesn't have to be concerned at a later time, about the tree the seed will become, because all seeds will produce trees and fruits after their own kind (Genesis 1:11-12). It was this same logic the devil used against Adam and Eve to corrupt the seed of God in them. He [devil] enticed Eve with a different fruit (Genesis 3:6), which looked pleasurable to the eyes but contained a different seed, instead of the one that had been sown by God initially.

Interestingly, when two different seeds are planted in the same soil, the latter seed has the tendency to corrupt the former by wrestling with it for space, time and nourishment (Leviticus 19:19). Hence, the seed of God in man now wrestles with the seed of the devil for survival.

This is a war we fight daily in our minds. All over the place we hear words that are targeted at our hearts, to corrupt the seed of God in us. We also see images around us aimed at producing wrong thoughts, there by bringing impure imaginations upon the soil of our hearts.

Regretfully, the devil now sows seeds of defilement throughout the internet; where pornography, vulgarity, violence, every evil thing becomes accessible at the tip of our fingers. Offering such convenience; making people comfortable with sin. Strategically, the devil targets our younger generation's minds with this same tool. You might be saying, "does this really matter?" Let me summarize.

The planting of the Seeds of defilement

"Now the works of the flesh are manifest, which are these; Adultery, fornication, uncleanness, lasciviousness, Idolatry, witchcraft, hatred, variance, emulations, wrath, strife, seditions, heresies, Envying, murders, drunkenness, revellings, and such like: of the which I tell you before, as I have also told you in time past, that they which do such things shall not inherit the kingdom of God."

-Galatians 5:19-21 KJV

Every seed replicates itself after its own kind. A seed actually looks innocent and insignificant in the way it appears at first, until eventually that seed becomes a tree and that tree becomes trees, and those trees start to form a large forest. The same thing applies to the seeds of defilement, which the devil seeks to sow in us daily. They start as something small, yet defiled, and produce more and more of the same. Just ponder on that for a minute.

Since the fall of man in the Garden of Eden, the seeds of defilement had been planted, they have been passed from generation to generation multiplying. It is therefore your responsibility to do everything you can, as to resist the devil from planting these seeds. Even to the point of uprooting any you may have already planted in your own heart.

This book will introduce you to what the seeds of defilement are and how you can guard your heart, live victoriously, and rise above the target of the devil.

"That which is born of the flesh is flesh; and that which is born of the Spirit is spirit"

-John 3:6 KJV

SEEDS OF DEFILEMENT

PART ONE
SEED OF LUST

"Thou shalt not sow thy vineyard with divers' seeds: lest the fruit of thy seed which thou hast sown, and the fruit of thy vineyard, be defiled."

DEUTERONOMY 22:9 KJV

"You are worthy, O Lord, to receive glory and honor and power: for you created all things, and by Your will they exist and were created."

REVELATION 4:11 NKJV

CHAPTER ONE
SEED OF IDOLATRY

Do you know that everything in existence has its origin? Yes! The trees you see all around have their origin. The flowers with their beautiful fragrance and the ones with attractive colors have their origin as well. The animals you see everywhere have their origin. Even humans, have an origin.

"All things were made by Him [God]; and without Him was not anything made that was made."

John 1:3 KJV

In the same vein, evil, darkness and wickedness have their origin in the father of eternal darkness and doom-satan! Nothing good is found with satan. The Bible says that satan is the father of all liars (John 8:44), adulterer, idolaters, just to mention a few.

"And the serpent [satan] said unto the woman, ye shall not surely die: For God doth know that in the day ye eat thereof, then your eyes shall be opened, and ye shall be as gods, knowing good and evil."

Genesis 3:4-5 KJV

Do you see how satan targets to corrupt every good thing God made? And so, he deceived Eve in the Garden of Eden into eating God's forbidden fruit.

However, satan knows that every fruit has seeds in itself, which will grow into more fruits when planted in good soil. Hence, satan introduced into humanity, the seeds of defilement.

Since then, these seeds of defilement had begun to replicate into more dangerous and destructive seeds of sinful pleasure, including the seed of idolatry which will be discussed in this chapter.

What is Idolatry?

Idolatry is the worship of objects known as idols. Anything you esteem above God is a form of idolatry, irrespective of what it might be; a graven image, a passion, a craving or strong desire for what you want above God.

More so, idolatry is when something else receives the worship that is due to the Almighty God.

There is only one true God, who seeks to be worshipped alone. He wants to be honored and adored. He is the creator of the 'seen' and the 'unseen'. Nothing in the universe exists without His consent and everything that exists is subject to His ruler-ship.

God manifests Himself wherever He is being honored. Those who worship God have learned the art of honoring Him. Hence, He shows forth mightily in their situation and on their behalf.

Yet, some people have consciously or unconsciously created gods for themselves in their own hearts and in their life, which they worship.

Any practice of worship that is not unto the one and true God is idolatry.

Worship and Idolatry

I would like to make it clear to you that worship is not idolatry. Rather, the object of worship is what makes it idolatrous.

In worship, you show reverence to whatever or whoever is most inestimable in your life. It suffices to say that whatever or whoever is paramount to your existence deserves your worship.

Therefore, the essence of worship is to bring pleasure to the object of worship and in this regard, we should worship the only true God to bring Him pleasure. The Bible says;

"Thou art worthy, O Lord, to receive glory and honor and power: for thou hast created all things, and for thy pleasure they are and were created."

Revelation 4:11 KJV

The creator of the universe seeks our worship and that is the only thing we can give to Him, in exchange for the seed of life that He has given to us.

Worship becomes a seed of defilement when it is done to an object less than God. Thus, this form of worship becomes idolatry.

The Bible says;

"Their land also is full of idols; they worship the work of their own hands, that which their own fingers have made."

Isaiah 2:8 KJV

Do you see that? There are people who *worship the works of their own hands.* (Isaiah 2:8). This implies that there are people who give reverence that is due to God to things which they've made as gods for themselves.

These people are those who prioritize material gain, selfish desires, sensual cravings, and passions for what they want, above their creator. They become controlled by these things and end up living their life by the seed of defilement, called idolatry.

Idolatry is a seed of defilement that is sown in the heart, which can manifest in various ways. Such as when a person worships an idol in the form of a passionate pursuit of a career, profession, fame, money, power and so on. All these at the expense of God, bring about idolatry.

Please, do not get me wrong. I don't mean to say that a career pursuit or quest to move higher in your professional cadre is wrong. What I mean is, that when you esteem what you want to achieve or acquire above God, then that becomes an idol to you.

Lust produces Idolatry

Please realize that even the seed of defilement in root of Idolatry has another fragment in it. That fragment is called lust.

What is lust?

Lust is an intense desire and a strong attachment to something that you long to have by all means, with a willingness to relegate all other things including God, just to acquire your desire.

This type of desire is sensual, emotional and demonic. It is mostly for gratification of a short-lived pleasure, which has no eternal gain. The Bible says;

"Their end is destruction; their god is their stomach; their glory is in their shame. They are focused on earthly thing."

Philippians 3:19 CSB

The goodness of God is revealed in the beauty of nature, the essence of life, the peace in Christ and the joy of the Holy Spirit.

Yet, the lustful desires of people have robbed themselves of God's goodness, and most times, they end up in destruction.

Any craving in your heart for something more important to you than God is idolatry and you must therefore be careful of whatever catches your fantasy, which progressively might lead you away from God.

Watch out for that desire which keeps drawing you away from God towards things that do not reflect Him. This is a dangerous seed, waiting for a time to grow into manifestation.

Lust is a subtle seed of Idolatry

"But every man is tempted, when he is drawn away of his own LUST, and enticed. Then when lust hath conceived, it bringeth forth sin: and sin, when it is finished, bringeth forth death."

James 1:14-15 KJV

The most dangerous thing about lust is that it is a seed that defiles the heart but does not appear harmful at conception.

Ironically, seeds are not usually given consideration, probably because of their size which appears little and 'innocent'. Yet, a seed is enough to start a forest when it finds fertile ground to grow and thrive successfully.

This is also true of lust-a subtle seed of idolatry; this can entice anyone, until the person yields to its course, and finally falls into idolatry of lustful desires.

There is hope, the seed of lust can be terminated at inception, when you do not give it a viable condition for survival in your heart.

"And when he sowed, some seeds fell by the way side, and the fowls came and devoured them up."

Matthew 13:4 KJV

Apparently, not all seeds grow, when they are sown. Why is that? This simple illustration is an indication that for a seed to grow on soil, every condition for its survival must be favorable.

Similarly, the heart of man is the breeding ground for all sorts of seeds. But, it is the environment of the heart that determines if a seed will thrive successfully or not. Thankfully, it is in your capacity to either allow the seed of lust to survive and lead into idolatry or you destroy such a seed forever.

Furthermore, lust could appear as a simple desire that doesn't look harmful, a passion that does not look destructive or a sight that merely looks attractive. But then, it becomes detrimental, when it begins to draw you away from God in pursuit of something else that is less than God.

When you make God your all, everything else becomes your possession because, nothing exist outside of God. It is as simple as this;

"But seek ye first the kingdom of God, and his righteousness; and all these things shall be added unto you."

Matthew 6:33 KJV

Sadly, those who through lust seek after material things end up either having it with lack of fulfillment in life or they never have it and die struggling to obtain it.

It will interest you to know that the pursuit of God brings forth positive additions of every good thing in life.

Seed of Idolatry

Take for instance, when you plant a seed inside the soil, do you ever see the seed growing? Of course not! Nobody ever sees a seed growing under the soil. But definitely, you will know that the seed is growing when it shoots up above the soil surface. The same goes for the seeds of defilement - nobody sees them until they begin to grow into something bigger and uncontrollable.

Seeds fall upon our hearts through the things we hear, see and allow to settle within us. A seed of defilement is therefore any subtle, unnoticeable contamination of the heart that gradually takes root firmly in you, as you nurture it to growth in your heart.

The heart is the vital part of you which serves as the soil in which seeds of words, imaginations and thoughts grow. To protect the heart from such defilement, you have a responsibility to yourself. The Bible says;

"Keep thy heart with all diligence; for out of it are the issues of life."

Proverbs 4:23 KJV

The heart and the mind are intimately connected with God in the Bible. There is no pure life without a pure heart. Likewise, a defiled life sprouts from a defiled heart. The life we live outwardly is a reflection of the seed growing inwardly.

The heart has neither eyes nor ears of its own, so it feeds on what the eyes see and the ears hear and then processes it into thoughts and imaginations which when pondered upon, serve as nourishment to the seeds planted upon the heart.

Innocently, many allow the seeds of defilement to grow within them. It becomes too late to correct the effects before noticing the dangers.

No seed falls on your heart and grows, without your consent unless you allow it.

If you allow your heart to become a dumping ground for all forms of thoughts, words and imaginations, you'll inevitably choke to death the seed of God in you and replace it with seeds of defilement which will start to grow. The Bible says;

"Finally, brethren, whatsoever things are true, whatsoever things are honest, whatsoever things are just, whatsoever things are pure, whatsoever things are lovely, whatsoever things are of good report; if there be any virtue, and if there be any praise, think on these things."

Philippians 4:8 KJV

Therefore, any thought that contradicts the above scripture is a defilement of the heart.

"This know also, that in the last days perilous times shall come. For men shall be lovers of their own selves, covetous, boasters, proud, blasphemers, disobedient to parents, unthankful, unholy, Without natural affection, trucebreakers, false accusers, incontinent, fierce, despisers of those that are good, Traitors, heady, highminded, lovers of pleasures more than lovers of God;"

2 Timothy 3:1-4 KJV

These are the last days, people see serving God as something archaic, unnecessary. They want to be independent of their creator. You cannot survive these times without God. He is all you will ever need, and He will always be the only one you should ever want.

Today, so many people have substituted God for something less than Him. They take the things of God for granted and this does not glorify Him. Friend, nothing is more dangerous than this.

You need God today, tomorrow and forever. Whatever does not reflect God must not be found in you or around you because, everything about God is just, perfect and good (Genesis 1:31) and so are you.

Whatever competes with God in your heart is thus, idolatry.

The truth is, you cannot keep your gaze on lust and at the same time focus on God. The one you pay most attention to will grow with time.

Many have lusted on material possession so much that they've lost touch with God as their source and this brings us to a paramount area of idolatry-covetousness.

Covetousness is Idolatry

The word covetousness in the Hebrew word is translated as the word "*betsa*," which means 'to plunder', 'to acquire' or 'possess an insatiable desire for honest gain' (Exodus 18:21)

More so, the Greek word translated covetousness in the New Testament as 'greed,' 'setting the heart upon,' 'longing,' and 'lusting for.' The Bible says;

"Put to death therefore what is earthly in you; sexual immorality, impurity, passion, evil desire, and covetousness, which is idolatry."

Colossian 3:5 ESV

Covetousness rises from a desire. It comes from a strong desire to have something which is not yours but belongs to another. Hence, you go overboard to acquire these things.

Actually, God has made everything good. Therefore, desiring His goodness is not a wrong thing to do. A desire for a car, house, money and a whole lot of material things is not bad as it were. God really wants us to enjoy every good thing of life.

Yet, desires for these things, as though your life and the reason for your living depend on them makes it all wrong.

The Bible says;

*"Let your conversation be without covetousness; and be content with such things as ye have: for He hath said, **I will never leave thee, nor forsake thee.**"*

Hebrew 13:5 KJV

Hence, see God as your source. Hold Him by His promises and do not start a desperate search for something else, which might take your heart away from God.

Whatever God gives comes with an aura of peace and satisfaction. He wants you to be content with what you have that He [God] has given to you.

As a matter of fact, there is nothing you have that is not from God. When you understand this simple truth, you will no longer covet that which someone else has, which you do not have or cannot afford to get.

Covetousness causes a person to do dangerous things in order to acquire riches, fame and material possessions. This act of excessive desire for things is what makes covetousness idolatry.

Previously, we had seen that idolatry is not just about worship of graven images but an obsession for what you want that is not yours or that seems not to be yours.

Jesus Christ gave a stern warning in the Bible as regards covetousness, when He said;

"And he said unto them, Take heed, and beware of covetousness: for a man's life consist not in the abundance of the things which he possess."

Luke 12:15 KJV

The truth is, material possession doesn't spell out the essence of living. Whatever you have acquired irrespective of how much it is, you will one day relinquish everything. So why the desperation for material gains that will make you forget God?

In addition, the love for materialism has an effect on the heart of any person, resulting in obsession.

Obsession mostly comes with love, irrespective of the person or the thing you love. Therefore, the effect of obsession on material gain is the cause of idolatry through covetousness or sometimes called greed.

I would like to show the destructive effect of covetousness on certain individuals in the Bible.

Achan

"And Achan answered Joshua, and said, indeed I have sinned against the LORD God of Israel, and thus and thus have I done:

"When I saw among the spoils a goodly Babylonish garment, and two hundred shekels of silver, and a wedge of gold of fifty shekels weight, then I coveted them, and took them; and, behold, they are hid in the earth in the midst of my tent, and the silver under it."

Joshua 7:20-21 KJV

Achan and His family were destroyed because of Achan's greed. You can see how his mind is absolutely absent from anything else, except for the gold that he desires and the Babylonian garment that he loves.

This is an example that when covetousness rules your mind , it then becomes a seed which will one day grow into a destructive object of worship.

Judas Iscariot

Judas Iscariot is another prime example having an object of greed, even despite being an disciple.

The Bible says;

"This he said, not that he cared for the poor; but because he was a thief, and had the bag, and bare what was put therein."

John 12:6 KJV

What a pity! An unbridled desire brought down a man of such stature and status.

Invariably, we can see that covetousness starts as a seed of intense desire, until it becomes an idol of destruction.

Watch Out! A seed might have been planted

A seed of lust doesn't appear dangerous and that's a danger in itself. It comes with a beautiful coat yet deadly poison. It comes as busyness of daily activities, yet, draws you away from God.

Take note of these things; when your attention begins to shift from your service to God.

When the things of God, which usually inspire you, no longer do. Or your desire has become fixed on materialism more than on God, in all these, check it out! A seed might have been planted which you have not taken cognizance of.

A seed of lust might come as a simple desire yet, idolatry creeps in gradually. Watch out therefore, for any desire that hinders your pursuit for God and brings you to a form of activity that reduces God to nothing in your life. Ensure you keep idols, lust, covetousness away from your mind and heart.

SPIRITUAL NUGGET 1

Falling away" simply means that people turn away from faith in God and begin to trust other things. These other things become idols in their hearts- "golden calves" which they depend upon to lead them through this life and then into heaven.

"Marriage is honorable among all, and the bed undefiled; but fornicators and adulterers God will judge ..."

HEBREWS 13:4 NKJV

CHAPTER TWO
SEED OF FORNICATION

One of the most pleasurable experiences in human existence and mutual relationship is sex. When you hear the word "sex", what comes to your mind? How do you feel?

The reality is, this word has gained so much popularity today more than any time in human history. From bill boards, commercials, social media and internet adverts; regardless of what is being sold, from body creams to exotic cars; almost everything everywhere is coated with a gel of "sex-appeal".

Good news! We didn't just evolve, we were created. The creator of the Earth has laid down principles that are made available in His "word". These principles are not impediments to sweeter, better, productive and pleasurable life; rather they exist to give genuine meaning, protection and purpose to our earthly existence and daily experience.

Among many of life's issues and human activities; the intimacy (*Koinonia* in Greek) between a man and a woman, holds a very important place in the heart of God. This is because *Koinonia* is not only an experience that involves the body, spirit and soul but also a sacred vehicle that transports humans from the heavenly workshop of creation to earthly existence in form of a newborn.

Therefore, God has ordained a safe and fulfilling institution for acceptable and more enjoyable intimacy; it is called- marriage. Hence, intimacy in marriage becomes the only yardstick for pleasure, procreation and true intimacy.

What is Fornication?

Merriam-Webster dictionary defines fornication as a consensual sexual intercourse between two persons (male and female) not married to each other.

The emphasis on fornication is on the marital status of these two people.

More so, the act of fornication does not start with the act but in the heart.

Fornication Starts in the Heart

"Marriage is honorable in all, and the bed undefiled..."

Hebrews 13:4 KJV

Sexual intimacy in itself is not a sin. But, when it is not done within the boundary of marriage, then it becomes an act of defilement.

You should understand that fornication does not just happen. It is a process, just like all other seeds of defilement.

Fornication begins from the seed level (in your thoughts) and if not controlled, it can lead to the main act.

"Keep thy heart with all diligence; for out of it are the issues of life."

Proverbs 4:23 KJV

The Bible says; *keep your heart diligently*, not carelessly.

You should not allow your heart to wander or be controlled by the occurrences around. When you have good control over the seeds that are planted in your heart, then you already have a control over the actions of your life.

Amnon and Tamar

A major example of the seed of fornication is the incident that occurred between Amnon and Tamar in the Bible;

"Some time passed. David's son Absalom had a beautiful sister named Tamar, and David's son Amnon was infatuated with her.

Amnon was frustrated to the point of making himself sick over his sister Tamar because she was a virgin, but it seemed impossible to do anything to her.

Amnon had a friend named Jonadab, a son of David's brother Shimeah. Jonadab was a very shrewd man, and he asked Amnon, "Why are you, the king's son, so miserable every morning? Won't you tell me?"

Amnon replied, "I'm in love with Tamar, my brother Absalom's sister."

Jonadab said to him, "Lie down on your bed and pretend you're sick. When your father comes to see you, say to him, 'Please let my sister Tamar come and give me something to eat. Let her prepare food in my presence so I can watch and eat from her hand."

2 Samuel 13:1-5 CSB

Sadly, this was quite an unfortunate incidence because it was sexual intercourse between two siblings; the son and daughter of King David.

The Bible said that Tamar was fair. This means that she was very beautiful in appearance and Amnon could not help but to lust after his sister.

Nevertheless, Amnon's lustful feelings for Tamar could be because of the sensual intimacy between the two siblings. There were probably little or no restrictions between them when they were young as kids, and we could draw this conclusion because, even David did not rebuke Amnon when he requested that Tamar should come over to his chamber to serve him food.

More so, what made this situation unique was the presence of Jonadab; the friend of Amnon, whom the Bible described as a very subtle man.

Amnon could not express his feelings and thoughts until he told his friend. The friend's advice was all that Amnon needed to execute his lustful feelings towards his sister.

Learn from this...

The truth is the act of fornication that ensued between Amnon and Tamar was sponsored by Jonadab's advice to Amnon.

The lesson in this is the choice of the company or the friends you keep. Choose your friends wisely.

A common saying goes like this; *show me your friends and I will tell you who you are.*

The Bible also established that saying as;

"He that walks with wise men shall be wise: but a companion of fools shall be destroyed."

Proverbs 13:20 KJV

So, this was the case of Amnon, who had a bad friend, and it did not take long for him to exhibit the bad nature of his friend.

You see, you cannot be different from the company of friends you keep. Amnon yielded to his friend's advice on the step by step deception to lure his sister to bed.

Many good people with good intentions also fall victims of bad and defiling decisions, just because of the wrong company or friends they keep.

The truth of the matter is, your best friends cannot be prostitutes and you think you can keep yourself from fornication for long.

Paul puts it straight in I Corinthians 15 when he says;

"Be not deceived: evil communications corrupt good manners."

1 Corinthians 15:33 KJV

This implies that you must not deceive yourself. Take for instance; it is easier for the person at the foot of a ladder to drag the person at the top of the ladder down.

So it is with bad company. No matter how good mannered you are, take heed because you stand the risk of being corrupted by the wrong company of friends, who can lure you into defilement, especially the defilement through fornication as an adult.

Nevertheless, the act of fornication is a spontaneous act as nobody suddenly falls into fornication without its seed being planted in their heart first.

Therefore, let us consider some seed of fornication which when nurtured in the heart, can eventually grow into the act of fornication that causes defilement.

1. Idleness

Idleness is defined as a state where someone does not work or is not active.

You see, King David was vulnerable to the act of fornication because at the time when he ought to be busy in battle; he was at home idle; enjoying the view of the city.

A wise man once said; *an idle mind is the devil's workshop.* This is true.

In other words, when you do not engage your mind productively, regardless of how spiritual or powerful you may be, wrong thoughts tend to take over. Once the wrong thoughts take over your mind, the message is passed to the heart and the rest is history.

So, you should be careful what you do with every moment when you are less active or during your leisure time.

2. The Wrong things you watch and Read

Consequently, the things you read or watch interferes with your mind. What you watch is a form of information that goes into your mind, and if it is toxic to your mind, it tends to dislodge the good thoughts and images you already have.

Most people are used to reading books that stimulate their sexual urge and before long, they start to look for whom to practice with.

You need to avoid these things as they tend to lure you into illicit sex.

We are in a social media age, where all kind of junk is domiciled on the internet. Just a click or a search on the internet and whoops! You are on, watching all kinds of things in the comfort of your own home.

Sadly, a lot of youth have become sex addicts, simply because they indulge in constant exposure to pornography on the internet and have the habit of some erotic and or romance novels.

The truth is, you are what you read. This is because, what you read does not only inform you but you can end up being conformed to what you read.

A lot of people have spent time reading erotic magazines that teach them about masturbation and before long they are in the very act. This ends up becoming an addiction which poses serious danger to the individual involved in such act. But remember, it starts from the things you watch or read.

In addition, most teenagers have early exposure to the knowledge of sex and the urge to act on what they know. It begins from that point on especially if they are not well guarded.

Lesson from Job

The man Job in the Bible knew the effect of what he looked at and how it affected his thoughts and actions. In *Job 31:1*he said;

"I made a covenant with mine eyes; why then should I think upon a maid?

Subsequently, when you look at that verse you will expect Job to say that he made a covenant not to look at a maid. Rather, Job said that he has made a covenant not to think upon a maid.

Therefore, it implies that what you look at, becomes a though pattern and it is said that, *a man's life tends in the direction of his most dominant thoughts.*

So, when you see someone who fornicates for instance, you can draw a line back to how the person had fed his mind with inappropriate images, nudity and sexually provocative information over time.

3. Indiscipline

Indiscipline comes when someone lacks the control to abide by certain rules and the way to do things.

The keyword in the definition of 'indiscipline' is the lack of self-control.

You see the inability to say NO when you need to, especially when you already know the end result is deadly.

Take for instance King Solomon in the Bible. King Solomon had seven hundred wives and three hundred concubines (1kings 11:3).

This implies that he had a strong thirst for women and fornication through unbridled sex.

Some people are just like that. They have all the wealth and influence to attract women of all kind and they go all out with them.

More so, one common natural urge every normal human being has is the sexual urge. But, some people make sure they look for whom to have sex with each time the urge comes. That is a lack of self-control and indiscipline.

4. Wrong company

Another seed of defilement that spurs up fornication is wrong company.

This point had been stressed earlier in the story of Amnon and Tamar, how Jonadab who was Amnon's friend lured him into fornication.

The influence of the company of friends around you plays an important role in your life.

However, when you surround yourself with the right people, it becomes easier for you to make right decisions. And if unfortunately they are the subtle type like Jonadab, you might end up otherwise. Hence, watch out for the people in your circle of friends.

Nevertheless, no matter how terrible society becomes, you can escape the snare of fornication if you choose to.

Ways to prevent fornication

You may ask how can I keep myself from fornication in this generation where sex is totally free or how can someone be free from the act? The truth is, there is always a way out.

Below are some steps you can take to avoid fornication or to come out of its defilement.

Salvation

The Bible says;

"How shall we escape, if we neglect so great salvation; which at the first began to be spoken by the Lord, and was confirmed unto us by them that heard Him?"

Hebrews 2:3 KJV

Salvation is still the principal way out of the corruption of this age.

The level of exposure and the vulnerabilities in this generation is high, especially with the advent and improvements of the internet.

I overheard a discussion sometime back in a barber shop that there was an app that could be installed on mobile phones to place an order for prostitutes just the way you order for a taxi and the taxi driver comes to pick you up at your house.

How can we escape such increasing act of destruction except by salvation? Jesus declared in the book of *John 14:6;*

"Jesus saith unto him, I am the way, the truth, and the life..."

Nevertheless, the way out of such a deadly act of fornication is to come to Jesus. When you come to Jesus, all things become new and you'll receive the grace to withstand the pressure of illicit sex all around. The Bible says;

"For the grace of God that bringeth salvation hath appeared to all men,

Teaching us that, denying ungodliness and worldly lusts, we should live soberly, righteously, and godly in this present world;"

Titus 2:11-12 KJV

The grace needed to say no to the pressure of fornication and to come out of sexual addiction is available to anyone through salvation by the blood of Jesus.

There is none greater in this house than I; neither hath he kept back anything from me but thee, because thou art his wife: how then can I do this great wickedness, and sin against God?

Genesis 39:9 KJV

Joseph was a young man who saw a free opportunity to fornicate with Potiphar's wife. Yet, his heart for God was the main reason he said no.

The lesson here is simple. If you love God you will keep your body from defilement.

Renewal of mind

The eyes and the ears are the major gateways to the mind. To prevent fornication, you must filter what you allow into your mind through your eyes and your ears. The Bible says;

"And be not conformed to this world: but be ye transformed by the renewing of your mind, that ye may prove what is that good, and acceptable, and perfect, will of God."

Romans 12:2 KJV

The mind is the seat of all our actions. Whatever you do is first conceived in your mind. So, you have to ensure that your mind is in a pure state by constant renewal.

Every transformation in your life begins with the mind. The Bible admonishes that the mind must be renewed frequently, to keep it pure and healthy.

Regular study of God's word and teachings from anointed men of God is vital to renewing the mind. Subsequently, God's word removes the thought of fornication from your mind so you cannot be found in the act.

"And even as they did not like to ***retain God in their knowledge****, God gave them over to a reprobate mind, to do those things which are not convenient;"*

Romans 1:28 *KJV*

The scriptures make it clear that those who do not retain God in their knowledge end up with a reprobate mind.

The word 'reprobate' means to condone strongly an evil act. This means that the person who does not give his or her heart to God's word ends up with any kind of evil thoughts, which includes that of fornication.

When you daily clean your mind with God's word, you live above fornication.

Rather than reading magazines that teach you ways to fornicate and enhance your sexual urge, why not pick up anointed Christian literature and remove all those erotic novels from your library and place the knowledge of God there instead.

More so, you need to watch the kind of movies you view and the sites you visit on the internet, the contents of those things settle in your mind and corrupt it.

"Finally, brethren, whatsoever things are true, whatsoever things are honest, whatsoever things are just, whatsoever things are pure, whatsoever things are lovely, whatsoever things are of good report; if there be any virtue, and if there be any praise, ***think on these things.****"*

Philippians 4:8 KJV

The reality is that, it is only from God's word that you can find pure, true, honest, just, lovely and virtuous things to think about. Hence, develop a schedule for God's word and retain the knowledge of God in your mind.

Flee

"Flee fornication..."

1 Corinthians 6:18 KJV

To flee means to run swiftly away from danger. Paul admonishes the Corinthians and all children of God never to negotiate with fornication when it comes with its lustful desire but to take a decisive action to flee.

You choose to flee from that ungodly movies when you take the action to delete them from your mobile phone or remove them from your home.

Flee from that sexually provocative chat or talk. I want you to flee from all explicit or nude images. Flee from those friends that lure you into sin. Flee from those provocative vices.

Regardless of how demeaning society might be, endeavor to take a sharp and deliberate action to secure your soul.

The man who made an absolute U-turn from fornication in his generation is the man- Joseph. I will not cease to make reference to him.

Kindly read his experience as slowly and carefully as you can...You will be impacted by his resolute and wise attitude to the seed of fornication that was ceaselessly and heinously dispersed on the field of his good heart.

"And it came to pass after these things, that his master's wife cast her eyes upon Joseph; and she said, lie with me.

Gen 39:8 But he refused, and said unto his master's wife, Behold, my master knoweth not what is with me in the house, and he hath put all that he hath into my hand:

he is not greater in this house than I; neither hath he kept back anything from me but thee, because thou art his wife: how then can I do this great wickedness, and sin against God?

And it came to pass, as she spake to Joseph day by day, that he hearkened not unto her, to lie by her, or to be with her.

And it came to pass about this time that he went into the house to do his work; and there was none of the men of the house there within.

And she caught him by his garment, saying, lie with me: and he left his garment in her hand, and fled, and got him out."

-Genesis 39: 7-12 KJV

From the verses above, we see the wife of Potiphar talking to Joseph for a long time about fornicating with her and he kept refusing. On this very day, she met him alone in the house forced Joseph, this time he didn't discuss it with her like he had always done, the Bible says he left his garment and fled.

The garment to us can be some opportunities that demand we fornicate first, maybe as a lady your boss demands you to fornicate with him to gain promotion. Like Joseph, will you leave the promotion behind and flee for your life? Let it go and God will not just vindicate you but restore to you what you left behind.

In conclusion, ***Proverbs 6:26;*** *for by means of a whorish woman a man is brought to a piece of bread: and the adulteress will hunt for the* ***precious life***. KJV

Understand that your life is precious to God, you have a glorious and colorful destiny. The devil is aware so that is the reason for the struggles you face which is also why he is doing all he can to bring you down and reduce you to a piece of bread. You are special to God and you should carry that mentality, so you won't mess up your life. Your body is God's temple, where He dwells. That is the reason the devil is all out for your soul to defile the temple of God and send Him out of your life. Don't give in friends, to the wiles of the devil.

I pray in the name of Jesus that God will give you the grace to stand strong, to withstand all the pressure and temptations around and may you receive the grace to say NO when the need arises. May your life be pleasing to God from now on in Jesus name (Amen).

SPIRITUAL NUGGET 2

The greatest battle for a Christian today is the battle in their thought life. Be not deceived; God is not mocked; for whatsoever a man soweth, that shall he also reap. Think about this before you make your next decision.

"Do not mix with winebibbers or with gluttonous eaters of meat; for the drunkard and the glutton will come to poverty, and drowsiness shall clothe a man with rags."

PROVERBS 23:20-21 NKJV

CHAPTER THREE
SEED OF DRUNKENNESS

"And God said, Behold, I have given you every herb bearing seed, which is on the face of all the earth, and every tree, in the which is the fruit of a tree yielding seed; to you it shall be for meat....And God saw everything that he had made, and, behold, it was very good."

Genesis 1:29, 31

Awesome! Everything God created was good. The birds of the air, the fishes in the sea, the animals, the plants, even humans; everything was made by God perfectly.

God graciously put in the custody of mankind, everything He made, so that we can use it for our benefit. Then, it became so easy for humans to make use of animals for food and or recreation, the plants for clothing, food, shelter and drinks like alcohol.

Alcohol

Alcohol is an old manufactured product of mankind from plants. It is any form of intoxicating beverage with sometimes has a bitter or sweet aroma.

In fact, the nature of every alcoholic drink, either liquor or fine wine makes alcohol a drink that entices its drinker often.

This implies that, intake of alcohol always stir up a longing for more drinks. Hence, it harbors in it a tremendous power to control its drinker which leads to drunkenness.

What is drunkenness?

"Be not among winebibbers; among riotous eaters of flesh:

For the drunkard and the glutton shall come to poverty: and drowsiness shall clothe a man with rags... Who hath woe? Who hath sorrow? Who hath contentions? Who hath babbling? Who hath wounds without cause? Who hath redness of eyes? They that tarry long at the wine; they that go to seek mixed wine."

Proverbs 23:20-21, 29-30

Surprisingly, the above Bible verses perfectly describe the characteristics of someone habitually given to alcohol.

The Word Net dictionary describes a drunken person as one who is "made sottish, senseless, or infatuated by alcohol or wine.

How do you feel when you imagine a well-dressed, highly intelligent, educated and informed man...becoming so intoxicated with alcohol that he then wallows in the mud like a pig; after a visit to the bar on a Friday night? Awful, right?

For instance, this is what the seed of drunkenness can make any sane and right thinking individual do or become, when such a person yields to the subtle deception of the "taste" for alcohol.

Drunkenness is an Abuse

"And be not drunk with wine, wherein is excess..."

Ephesians 5:18

Abuse is an improper use of any substance. It is an excessive use of a thing that makes it lose its relevance or intended purpose.

In the case of wine, Paul admonished his son in the Lord, Timothy thus;

"Drink no longer water, but use a little wine for thy stomach's sake and thine often infirmities."

I Timothy 5:23

This implies that there could be a recommendation of a "*little wine*" only in the case of certain ailment.

The truth is, anything that exists can be abused, so also is wine or alcohol, in this case.

A thin line which separates drinks from drunkenness is abuse. How? You may ask. It is because drunkenness is an abuse of drinks, particularly, alcohol.

The way in- It starts with a seed

Drunkenness is like every other seed of defilement, it starts subtle.

Sometimes, it begins like a "seed of desire" to stimulate the body, to "feel among", "feel high", quench a thirst, eradicate a thought or a cheer crave to explore alcohol.

Other times, drunkenness could be as a result of social pressure, peer group influence and exposure to alcohol stimulating activity.

A short Story...

Just on a lighter mood, I will like to let you in on an interesting and intriguing story of a Minister of God.

This man of God was invited for a reunion party of old friends from his Alma matter. It was just right in the middle of the reunion party that some of these old friends persuaded him to take some "shots of alcohol."

Since this man of God could not resist the pressure from his old friends, he gave in and drank wine until he became drunk.

After the reunion party was over, he managed to get himself home, where he fell flat in his sitting room and slept it off.

Still in his almost unconscious state, his darling wife came in to see her husband well clothed but laid out on the ground. To relieve the man of God from his misery, his wife tried to pull down his trouser to allow him to rest well. The moment the wife tried to remove his belt, the man of God shouted; "Please do not do it, I am a minister of God, I am Married, I have kids, I love Jesus". So interesting! This man of God said all these subconsciously, without knowing that he was already with his wife at home.

Do you see how pressure from friends or social pressure could establish the seed of Drunkenness in virtually anybody?

Drowning your sorrows by drinking?

Let me ask you; can you solve a problem by creating another? Or let me ask you in this manner; will you kill the seed of drunkenness by more alcohol intake?

Of course not! Instead, the seed of drunkenness will receive more strength to grow the more you drink.

The belief that one can shut down his sorrows and sadness by "strong drink" is not only childish but also comical. Those who think they can dash away their miserable feelings by getting drunk are insincere. The best you can get from being drunk is a temporary relief, which will give way to greater depression even after the drunkenness is gone.

The seed of drunkenness grows to penury

"He that loves pleasure shall be a poor man: he that loves wine and oil shall not be rich".

Proverbs 21:17

Do you know that the seed of drunkenness is a quick way to poverty? Yes, it is.

Consider how much in dollars it will take a man to get drunk in a quarter of a year and you will appreciate the fact that drunkards might actually be drinking up their future and emptying it into the sewage pipes! Yet, alcohol can better be avoided than corrected.

More dangerous than alcohol is the praise of people that gets people intoxicated

Acts 12:22-23

Jesus attitude to the seed of drunkenness

Since Jesus provided good wine during the marriage at Cana, would He have stylishly planted or approved of the seed drunkenness in the people? Would He have promoted alcoholism, knowing that it would pull people far away from the cause He came to die for?

We know that Jesus Himself warned believers against the possibility of getting drunk. In His message, he said that drunkenness should not be allowed in the believer's life.

And take heed to yourselves, lest at any time your hearts be overcharged with surfeiting, and drunkenness, and cares of this life, and so that day come on you unawares."

-Luke 21:34

He could not have approved of what He told the people will debar them from heaven.

A Christian cannot be a drunkard and a drunkard can only be a Christian after he/she has become born again. In fact, Paul admonished the Christians in Time

"Let us walk honestly, as in the day; not in rioting and drunkenness, not in chambering and wantonness, not in strife and envying". Rom 13:13, and to the Corinthian church, he wrote:

"But now I have written to you not to keep company, if any man that is called a brother be a fornicator, or covetous, or an idolater, or a reviler, or a drunkard, or an extortionist; with such an one no not to eat".

1Corinthians 5:11

It was so serious in the Old Testament Scriptures that not a single priest or Levite was permitted by God to taste any form of strong drink else such a Levite loses his right to priesthood! How much more the believers of today with a higher calling, greater grace and opportunities?

The power of addiction

Fully grown seed of drunkenness manifests in addiction.

Addiction to alcohol starts from the thought (seed) to an occasional sip, to a regular glass, and then to bottles until the drinker becomes addicted to drunkenness.

At this stage, the seed has grown to become a tree with branches; the drinker is subjected to partial or full control by alcohol.

The truth is, anything you become so fond of has a certain level of control over you. Friend, when you allow the seed of drunkenness to grow and have tentacles in you, then you are an addict to alcohol. You will also lose control of yourself.

Addiction to wine or alcohol has destroyed many lives and homes.

"At the last it bites like a serpent, and stings like an adder. Your eyes shall behold strange women, and your heart shall utter perverse things. Yes, you shall be as he that lies down in the middle of the sea, or as he that lies on the top of a mast.

They have stricken me, shall you say, and I was not sick; they have beaten me, and I felt it not: when shall I awake?

I will seek it yet again"

Proverbs 23:32-35

Addiction to alcohol causes depression, anxiety, personality disorder, loss of self-esteem and compulsive comportment. This is apart from health problems that have been medically proved to be related to alcohol.

Apart from the numerous psychosocial problems that drunkenness can cause, the Alcohol Rehab Guide.org reports that the heart is at the mercy of adverse effects of alcohol consumption. When it is consumed over a time, alcohol has the potential of weakening the heart, hindering the flow of oxygen and nutrients to other vital organs in the body. It is reported that regular and excessive intake of alcohol increases the fats in the blood vessels which can contribute to the risk of developing complicated health conditions like heart disease and diabetes.

The Seed of drunkenness relegates and debases

Have you ever thought of why God restrained the Biblical Nazarite from drinking alcohol right from the womb of their mothers? It was because drunkenness reduces the honour and integrity of its victim. God did not want the seed of drunkenness to be planted in the yet to be born Levite by his mother. Since a priest must be a man of utmost piety and decorum, alcohol has a ready-made sting against man's integrity.

A drunkard is naked and bereft of ideas

Generally, wines are made from seeds and fruits. This is the way God created it. But there are divine guidelines on how all that He created should be used. In the Garden of Eden, Adam and Eve were commanded not to eat of the tree of the knowledge of good and evil, lest they die. They did eat and the seed was planted in them, but it was to their disadvantage.

"And the eyes of them both were opened, and they knew that they were naked; and they sewed fig leaves together, and made themselves aprons".

Genesis 3:7

When the seed of drunkenness grows, it makes one spiritually naked and bereft of where and how to proceed. It clouds your vision and impairs your thoughts. It breeds irresponsibility and takes away sobriety, reducing the drunkard to an object of ridicule and shame.

Noah's mistake through the seed

Learn from the story of Noah. Prosperity, grace and favor can be very tempting. Noah's prosperity was a problem for his family. He planted the seeds in his vineyard, processed it and drank to stupor. The seed of drunkenness took charge and Noah lost control of himself and his family.

"And Noah began to be an husbandman, and he planted a vineyard: And he drank of the wine, and was drunken; and he was uncovered within his tent".

Genesis 9:20-21

Noah did not only bring open shame on himself, he also brought a perpetual curse on his son, Ham through his drunkenness. Little wonder why the grandson of Ham, Nimrod was the builder of Babel, where men started a revolt against God, the Creator.

In Proverbs 20:1, *we see that: "Wine is a mocker, strong drink is raging: and whosoever is deceived thereby is not wise".* This means a drunkard is a fool as long as he remains so.

Lot's incest through the seed of drunkenness

Have you ever been influenced by alcohol to make decisions before? You would have seen later that the decisions taken under the power of wine were, most times, very unreasonable and even foolish. Some actions are regretted for life. Such was the incest committed by Lot due to drunkenness

"Come, let us make our father drink wine, and we will lie with him, that we may preserve seed of our father.

And they made their father drink wine that night: and the firstborn went in, and lay with her father; and he perceived not when she lay down, nor when she arose.

And it came to pass on the morrow, that the firstborn said unto the younger, Behold, I lay yesternight with my father: let us make him drink wine this night also; and go thou in, and lie with him, that we may preserve seed of our father.... Thus were both the daughters of Lot with child by their father."

Genesis 19:32-36

Have you caved in under the seed of drunkenness to take wrong steps? Lot's daughters knew the power of excess wine to make one act against the right standard and personal integrity. They needed to conceive and have children and there was no man on hand. To them, they must act fast by appealing to the seed of drunkenness in their father, Noah. And how would they make their father do it except by making him drunk?

Which is better, moderate or no alcohol at all? Sincerely, the answer is no alcohol at all. It has been discovered that if you don't drink alcohol at all, you will have a relaxed body that is devoid of unnecessary agitation and disturbances.

Those who choose to drink moderately but regularly provide basis for relationship crisis, nervousness, melancholic behavior, restlessness, and emotional problems.

Of course more complicated scenarios are encountered by drunkards.

Deliver yourself from the seed and its "taste"

Friend, there is no "window dressing" here. Know the truth and it will make you free. Drunkenness is a serious problem and getting addicted to it is calamitous if not urgently dealt with. Dealing with the problem requires deliberate efforts on the part of the victim.

I believe you are surprised at the word "victim". Yes, and frankly too, a drunkard is a victim of the orchestrations of Bacchus, the god of wine.

When people that are given to drunkenness tell you they are in control, don't believe them. On the contrary, they are under the influence of a toxic wine, Bacchus. Nonetheless, it is their willingness to surrender their control that subjects them to Bacchus's influence.

The good news is: a clean and clear break from drunkenness is possible, even as you are reading this book.

"For there is hope of a tree, if it be cut down, that it will sprout again, and that the tender branch thereof will not cease".

Job 14:7

There is hope. The drunkard can be completely set free from the seed of drunkenness.

Follow me as I take you through the steps to freedom

I. Know the problem

"Behold, I was shaped in iniquity; and in sin did my mother conceive me".

Psalm 51:5

This is the most difficult step on the ladder to freedom from drunkenness. Even in the very state of stupor, only a handful will agree they are drunk! And only a very few will agree that the seed of drunkenness resides in them.

If you desire total freedom from the power of alcohol, the first thing is to see it as a serious personal problem from which you need an urgent help. Good enough, when this realization is exhibited by the victim, the solution is near. God values personal realization and sincere confession.

ii. Know the Saviour

"And you shall know the truth, and the truth shall make you free".

John 8:32

Do you remember that Jesus Himself provided enough and better wine at the marriage ceremony He attended at Cana of Galilee? You need to establish a walking and close relationship with Jesus, the Provider of truly nourishing wine, not some intoxicating brew.

A drunkard needs to experience salvation in Christ. How?

"That if you shall confess with your mouth the Lord Jesus, and shall believe in your heart that God has raised him from the dead, you shall be saved. For with the heart man believes to righteousness; and with the mouth confession is made to salvation".

"Romans 10:9, 10

By confessing your sins to Him, repenting of the sins and accepting His Lordship, your freedom begins in absolute terms. This must be done with the readiness to have a clean and a clear break from drunkenness.

iii. Kill the drunkenness seed

Self-denial is a sign of growth and maturity. To kill a passion is not as easy and simple as it appears. It involves *killing or crucifying* the flesh (the seed) by denying it what it craves for. Paul counseled

"For if you live after the flesh, you shall die: but if you through the Spirit do mortify the deeds of the body, you shall live". Rom 8:13

Living in true freedom from the seed of drunkenness demands that you mortify the deeds (works, cravings, lusts, preferences) of the body.

iv. Know who you are, where you are and where you should be

Nobility is usually lost when it associates with misdemeanor. Do you frequently see the crème de la creme of society drinking themselves to stupor in public glare? Hardly! A drunkard knows not his worth or value since naturally drunkenness devalues the human personality.

The point I am making here is that having been saved by Jesus, you now become a son or daughter of the Almighty God. You cannot, henceforth, stoop so low as to drift into alcoholism. That would be too demeaning!

v. Know the devil's strategy

Drunkenness is not a function of wealth. You might not have taken cognizance of this, but it is true. Many times, the devil's sinful opportunities are free. When it is going against the will of God, such as drunkenness; even without a penny, someone who "cares' can freely order alcohol for you. That is the devil's strategy.

You are to *"Abstain from all appearance of evil".* (1Thessalonians 5:22) and shun all pulls to drunkenness.

Except for those who commit suicide, I do not think a normal person will deliberately drink poisonous substance. As you become a Christian, drunkenness should naturally become as if poison!

Don't drop your fish at the river bank. The scent and aura of the flowing river can pull it back to the ocean and there it goes. Don't cherish your previous state of drunkenness. Don't cherish the brand or the bottle

Avoid reveling and the pub life. Maintain a clear and a clean break.

vi. Tame the Taste

The vegetarian diet is simply wonderful. But for those who cannot do without beef, the vegetarian is missing a splendid taste of meat. Actually, in reality, it is not so. Your taste bud gets used to what you consume over a considerable length of time.

Is alcohol always pleasant to taste? Most alcoholic drinks taste bitter, yet to its drinkers, it is the most pleasant taste ever. So, tame your taste and train it to consume things that are godly and healthy.

You can destroy the seed of drunkenness, even now. You can!

SPIRITUAL NUGGET 3

When the seed of drunkenness grows, it makes one spiritually naked and bereft of where and how to proceed. It clouds your vision and impairs your thoughts."

"Blessed is the man that walks not in the counsel of the ungodly, nor stands in the path of sinners, nor sits in the seat of the scornful"

PSALM 1:1

CHAPTER FOUR
SEED OF IMMORALITY

I am so glad that you've made it thus far with this book; SEEDS OF DEFILEMENT. So, I want to welcome you once again to another insightful and inspiring chapter of this book, as we have considered various life transforming chapters of the seeds of defilement in this book. I can assure you; this chapter of the book will not be anything less than the original intent which is to transform lives.

This book is carefully put together to give you an exposition on the seeds of defilement and the victory you have to destroy these seeds, even as a believer.

Truthfully, you have learnt in the previous chapters how the seeds of defilement took over humanity and how each act of sin is a seed sown into the heart of mankind by the devil right from the beginning of creation.

In this chapter, 'Seed of Immorality', the focus will be a critical examination of the root cause of immorality in its entirety and not just the aftermath of the act, but its source, as it affects many areas of life, which range from sex and sexuality to money, discipline, leadership, family and so on. I will also show you how God wants you to be victorious over immorality and the provisions He has made available for you.

Good News...

I have good news for you. God does not hate you. This is a truth that cannot be denied because God cherishes you above all of His creatures. You are created in the image of God (Genesis 1:26) and you are loved by Him. However, what God hates is not you but any act of immorality He [God] sees around you.

What is Immorality?

Merriam-Webster dictionary describes immorality as unlawful, unethical, sinful, evil among others. Not morally good or right, morally evil or wrong. This implies that immorality is said to be a behavior or an act that do not agree with the standard of right behavior by most people.

The above description does not limit immorality to just sexual perverseness as some people thought it to be. Immorality covers all acts that are considered unlawful, not just based on societal acceptance but much more importantly based on the word of God which remains the universal standard of living.

The seed of Immorality is inherent in human nature

The seed of immorality is deep seated in human nature. For instance, take an innocent new born as a case study. Nobody tells the child how to inflict pain on people by biting. The child is born with that intrinsic act.

Also, I want you to look at the story of Cain and Abel. They were the first set of human on the earth and so Cain killed his brother, Abel. Permit me to ask you, where did Cain learn that from? How was he able to add up the fact that he can take a fellow man's life? So, this also points to the fact that the seed of immorality is inherent in the human nature.

Apostle Paul lamented about this in Romans 7:21, 23;

"I find then a law, that, when I would do good, evil is present with me.

But I see another law in my members, warring against the law of my mind, and bringing me into captivity to the law of sin which is in my members"

Paul's desire was to do good and only the right thing, what is generally acceptable to God and society, but he observed that each time he wants to do good, evil suggestions also comes. So, he found himself struggling between doing good and evil.

That was the seed of immorality, which always seek to express itself in Apostle Paul, each time he wants to take a right step. This is another indication that regardless of who you are, the seed of immorality is something you must fight against daily.

Root of the Seed

The truth is, nobody just arrives at a particular destination suddenly. If there is an end there is obviously a beginning.

Cain did not just end up as a murderer. There was a source that 'sponsored' Cain's immoral act.

Therefore, I will let you in on some examples of men and women from scripture, who ended up in some sort of immorality, with emphasis on how they arrived at such an immoral destination at some point in their life.

1. Lucifer

What comes to mind when you hear of Lucifer? Of course! The devil himself. In Ezekiel 28, he was described as the anointed Cherub, covered with precious stones, the topaz, Sardis, diamond, onyx among others. In fact, verse 15 says that he was perfect from the day that he was created; perfect means no amendment, no blemish and no flaws. That was the kind of person that Lucifer was.

But, a day came and he [Lucifer] wanted to be like God; the 'created' who attempted to take the place of the 'creator'. This made him draw two-thirds of the Angels in heaven to himself, just to disrupt the peace in heaven.

The root of this very act of immorality is "pride". God looked at Lucifer and asked a serious question in Isaiah 14:12;

"How art thou fallen from heaven, O Lucifer, son of the morning? How art thou cut down to the ground, which didst weaken the nations"

It was as if God asked him again; how did you become so corrupt with all the investments in you.

Lucifer allowed pride into his heart and that was enough to bring him down.

"I will ascend above the heights of the clouds; I will be like the most High"

-Isaiah 14:14

What a suicidal thought! Lucifer became so filled with pride that he was no longer comfortable with being a Cherub anymore. He wanted to be like the most High God.

Pride they say comes before the fall. The root of such an evil act that led to Lucifer's displacement from heaven was pride. He felt nobody was like him among all the creatures of God.

Many today have also made some decisions in life that has led to their downfall. Simply, because they've allowed the seed of pride to grow in them. However, there is always a way out and that is why you are reading this book now.

2. Samson

Samson depicts strength and vigor, single handedly he judged Israel for twenty years without an army or team of elders or council members. He went alone to war and delivered Israel from their enemy as one man. All attempts to bring him down proved abortive. No effort by the Philistines was strong enough to weaken this supernaturally endowed man.

But then with all his strength there was a seed of sexual immorality that wrecked his ministry. He traveled to Gaza and saw a harlot and that same day he slept with her. And she later became the bait that was used to bring him down.

"Then went Samson to Gaza, and saw there an harlot, and went in unto her"

-Judges 16:1

The root of this immoral act was his **"lack of self-discipline** "for sexual desire. He could not resist the beauty of Delilah and that was the beginning of his fall. He could not look away after seeing her beauty.

Our ability to see what is wrong and look away especially when it is not right is self-discipline. This same is also attributed to King David, a man after God's heart.

"And it came to pass in an evening tide, that David arose from off his bed, and walked upon the roof of the king's house: and from the roof he saw a woman washing herself; and the woman was very beautiful to look upon"

-2 Samuel 11:2

David also saw Bathsheba and could not turn his eyes away until he slept with her. Paul said all things are lawful but not all are expedient. Self-discipline says NO when the action will lead to immorality.

3. Judas Iscariot and Gehazi

Judas was one of the main disciples hand-picked by Jesus and worked directly with him during His ministry on the earth. For about three years he prayed with Jesus, ate with Him, he was sent out also on evangelism and came back with the report of casting out devils. Judas was infact not just an ordinary member of the disciples, he was graciously given the responsibility of the treasurer (John 13:29; for some *of them* thought, because Judas had the bag...)

But when Jesus was to be betrayed, he was the instrument the devil used. So how did Judas also drop to such an immoral act?

At the root of his immorality was "***Greed***'. The Bible says he was stealing from the money of the ministry. While others were comfortable with the blessing of God on their life, Judas stole consistently from the bag.

"... But because he was a thief, and had the bag, and bare what was put therein."

John 12:6

This was not enough for him and he felt he needed more money, probably to pay some household bills and the next thing he did was to negotiate and auction his master for sale at the cost of thirty pieces of silver. He had a strong desire to have more even if it meant killing the Son of God.

Gehazi

Gehazi is also another high prospect. He served Elisha and was supposed to take over the ministry after Elisha but rather he inherited leprosy for his entire generation. Naaman has just been cleansed of leprosy and he came to Elisha to present gift unto him, Elisha rejected the gift and the Bible says Gehazi thought of it in his heart.

"But Gehazi, the servant of Elisha the man of God, said, Behold, my master hath spared Naaman this Syrian, in not receiving at his hands that which he brought: but, as the LORD liveth, I will run after him, and take somewhat of him"

- 2Kings 5:20

The immorality of Gehazi made him to lie against his master just to collect the gift and also when he got back with the gift he lied to his Master that he never went anywhere. All these came as a result of the root of ***Greed*** in him. He also wanted more than his master was giving him just like Judas Iscariot.

You should be content with the blessing of God on your life per time, never to move ahead of God. He makes all things beautiful in his time, at the right time you will also emerge to greatness; you will own that thing you are trying to steal.

Therefore, uproot every seed of immorality in your heart manifesting as greed. Greed is the capital foundation behind kidnapping and armed robbery, some people want to have it all at once without waiting for God's timing and process.

I pray that God will grant you the spirit of contentment which the Bible says is of great gain in Jesus name. Amen.

4. Hophni and Phinehas

These were the sons of Eli, they were the priest of the Lord. They served in the temple alongside their father. They held onto the highest honour in Israel after the king, they were honored to be born into the priestly lineage. They did not have a farm neither did they plant crops. All they needed was brought to them in the temple by the people especially during the yearly sacrifices.

Now the sons of Eli were sons of Belial; they knew not the LORD.

-1Samuel 2:12

These same sons knew not the Lord; they were forcefully taking flesh brought for sacrifices from the people without following due process. The Bible said they abhorred the offering of the Lord. They even slept with women that came to the tabernacle. Their immorality was great before the Lord (2Samuel 2:17).

These very things cost them their lives the same day the entire lineage of Eli was expunged from the priesthood of Israel, no old man will ever be seen or heard of in their family.

But how did these two sons who were previously called the priest of the Lord descend so low in immorality?

"... Notwithstanding they hearkened not unto the voice of their father..."

1Samuel 2:25

At the root of their immoral act as priest of the Lord was "Poor upbringing". Their father indulged them in wrong behavior even when they were young and it was too late when they came to the lime light. God didn't blame them alone for disregarding his altar but blamed Eli, their father also for their mess.

"... and honorest thy sons above me, to make yourselves fat with the chiefest of all the offerings of Israel my people?"

1Samuel 2:29

Today we hear of teenagers going to school and killing their fellow students with guns probably because they were offended. Young boys and girls in clubs, smoking and dealing drugs all because they lack adequate and quality upbringing.

"Train up a child in the way he should go: and when he is old, he will not depart from it"

Proverbs 22:6

When you train up a child in the right way while he is yet a child, what you are doing is uprooting every seed of immorality that may be inherent in such a child.

How to overcome Immorality

What then is the way out of immorality or better still, how can I watch my steps from afar so as not to fall into the destructive trap of immorality?

1. Yielding to the Warnings of the Holy Spirit

No sane parent would be glad to see his child in trouble or misbehaving, in the same way it is never the desire of God for us to fall into the temptation of immorality. He wants our life to bring glory to his name always, the same way our earthly parents would be glad to see us represent the name of the family well anywhere we go. God who sees the end from the beginning always warn us ahead of time before we fall into such an evil act. Let's us consider the case of Cain in Genesis 4:7;

"If thou doest well, shalt thou not be accepted? And if thou doest not well, sin lieth at the door. And unto thee shall be his desire, and thou shalt rule over him"

God warned him ahead of time that sin was lying at the door waiting to take over, that is to tell him that path he is treading will lead him to take a wrong step. Do not wait till you have fallen into immorality before you start to look for the solution.

Prevention they say is better than cure. Do not shut down the inner voice telling you to stop that evil plan. We have the Holy Spirit today to warn us and even show us the repercussions of our actions if we go through with them. Jesus also warned Peter that he would deny him three times, but Peter was too confident in himself and didn't bother asking Jesus if there was anything, he could do so he wouldn't deny him. Always yield to the Spirit of God in you.

2. Right Positioning

"Blessed is the man that walketh not in the counsel of the ungodly, nor standeth in the way of sinners, nor sitteth in the seat of the scornful"

Psalm 1:1

Where you position yourself determines what comes to you. You cannot go from work and reside in the bars and clubs yet be surprised that you are inhaling cigarette smoke or that you start to develop an appetite for alcohol. If you are always found among immoral people, you may end up in immoral acts too. Solomon gave some advice also in this regard.

"My son, if sinners entice thee, consent thou not. If they say, Come with us, let us lay wait for blood, let us lurk privily for the innocent without cause:

My son, walk not thou in the way with them; refrain thy foot from their path"

Proverbs 1:10-11, 15

Don't associate yourself with people whose aim is to always do evil. Run far from them. Change your association and immorality will drop off your life.

3. Choose Morality always.

"... that I have set before you life and death, blessing and cursing: therefore choose life, that both thou and thy seed may live:

Deuteronomy 30:19

One of the powers that God has placed in man is freewill. Every man has a will. You can determine to a great extent what to do and what not to do. Even salvation as beneficial as it is, is never forced on anyone. He made it an open platform for whosoever wills. The same plays out in this verse above, Moses encouraged the children of Israel to choose life, in this immoral world and corrupt society where doing the wrong thing is celebrated, you have an option to choose good or evil. The resultant effect of evil will always bring destruction while that of good will bring peace. At any junction where life presents you with right or wrong believe you have the power to choose the right action.

4. Develop a pure motive

Doing the right thing with an evil intention in the sight of God is the same as doing the wrong thing, because the same judgment comes on you. But when you train yourself by the help of the Holy Spirit to develop a pure motive for all your actions you will always be seen doing the right thing. Allow the word of God to shape your motive always. Let your action be love motivated, let it be a blessing to humanity. Don't defraud people for economic gain.

5. Go for Godly counsel.

"For by wise counsel thou shalt make thy war: and in multitude of counsellorsthere is safety"

- Proverbs 24:6

In the midst of Godly counsel you tend to take right decision. Are you held bound by some addictions and you have tried all you can to be free all to no avail? Seek counsel from men or women of God with proven Biblical testimony because iron sharpens iron.

In conclusion, you must understand that living above immorality is very possible, you have the Spirit of God to help you in all decisions and the grace of God is also freely available to help you say NO to immorality and YES to purity.

I pray that everything that is defiling in your life is broken, all yokes and addictions are destroyed in Jesus Name. Amen.

SPIRITUAL NUGGET 4

Doing the right thing with an evil intention in the sight of God is as good as doing the wrong thing, because the same judgment comes on you.

"But I say unto you, that whoever looks at a woman to lust for her has already committed adultery with her in his heart"

-MATTHEW 5:28

CHAPTER FIVE
SEED OF ADULTERY

I appreciate you for this wonderful step you have taken to read further. Assuredly, you will be glad that you did not stop reading, as this chapter will be the last of the first part of this book. So, be expectant!

Subsequently, I want to believe from the previous chapters, you have understood how the devil sows the seeds of defilement in the heart of mankind, such that they began to reflect the product of this seed in the form of idolatry, fornication, drunkenness and immorality of all kinds.

These seeds of defilement have been a battle for mankind for so long. However, this book in your hand is divinely engrafted with the truth from God's word to enlighten you on how to be totally free from the defilement of the devil.

In this chapter, we will consider another seed of defilement which the devil mostly uses to target families. This is the seed of Adultery.

Consider this...

Have you ever felt intimate with someone else besides your spouse? Maybe as a married man you've began to develop a sense of attraction towards a female colleague at work or as a married lady, you feel 'comfortable' in the warmth of another man who isn't your husband? Trust me, I have not come to judge you and I will never. I really want you to see the truth for yourself on how you can keep the devil away from your marriage or your marital relationship.

However, the feeling of attractiveness towards someone else who isn't your spouse or your partner is a lustful craving, which is periodic and can lead to regret if you yield to your feelings by taking action in the direction of your feelings.

In fact, you should not live your life by the way you feel per time. Feelings are not stable. It is just a rush of emotions that must be under control especially when it is towards a member of the opposite sex who isn't your spouse.

Take for instance, would you because of an urge for sex began to find a way to satisfy your feeling simply because your wife or husband isn't around? Or would you because of your sexual desire break your marital vow with a stranger other than your legally married spouse?

God's intention for intimacy in marriage

"For this reason a man will leave his father and mother and be joined to his wife, and the two will become one flesh."

-Matthew 19:5

God's intention for intimacy in marriage is to create continuation and oneness. He [God] wants the husband and wife to be open to one another and swim in harmony.

You will agree with me that only few understand the purpose of intimacy in marriage. Some people were made to believe that intimacy is an evolutionary accident. Therefore, they assume that intimacy is permitted anywhere and anyhow, as long as it is between consenting adults. But, that approach is naïve.

Then, why did God create Intimacy?

Perhaps the most obvious of God's purposes for intimacy and marriage is for reproduction. The Bible says;

"So God created man in His own image; in the image of God He created him; MALE AND FEMALE He created them"

-Genesis 1:27

The obvious truth is that *God* created both gender for intimacy; it isn't an evolutionary accident.

The simple and often overlooked answer to the question of intimacy is that *God created intimacy and marriage as one.* His reasons for doing so are nothing short of wonderful. Ignorance of God's purpose for intimacy has brought about enormous problems, which includes but is not limited to adultery.

Adultery is one of the worst things that can happen to a marriage and violates everything you've built with your partner in such a painful way. Many of us who have been a victim to an adulterous affair did not see it coming.

What is Adultery?

According to Oxford English Dictionary, Adultery is sexual intercourse by a married person with someone other than their spouse.

"You shall not commit adultery."

-Exodus 20:14

God's disposition is "no intimacy before marriage and outside marriage". Therefore, committing adultery is like compromising God's standard for marriage.

Adultery is one of the easiest ways to damage a relationship. Sometimes the damage could be so heavy that the marriage can seem damaged beyond repair. The reason adultery is so hard to walk through is because it destroys trust, which is the foundation to any healthy and true marital relationship.

Adultery can collapse even the strongest bonds and destroy your relationship from the inside out.

World Statistics on Adultery

Adultery is no longer a crime in any European country. Among the last Western European countries to repeal their laws were Italy (1969), Malta (1973),Luxembourg(1974), France (1975), Spain (1978), Portugal (1982), Greece (1983), Belgium(1987), Switzerland (1989), and Austria (1997).

As of 2017, the US states with laws against Adultery are Arizona, Florida, Kansas, Illinois, Massachusetts, Oklahoma, Idaho, Michigan, Wisconsin, Minnesota, Utah, New York, Mississippi, Georgia, North Carolina, South Carolina, and Maryland. However, they aren't generally enforced any more.

Kinds of Adultery

There are three kinds of Adultery you Probably Didn't Know about

Spiritual: This form of adultery doesn't involve unfaithfulness to your partner, but unfaithfulness to God. It really has to do with having an excessive attachment to things of the world.

Spiritual adultery includes any form of idolatry and that was a major theme throughout the Old Testament.

The Bible says;

"Thou shall love the LORD thy GOD with all your heart, and with all your soul, and with your entire mind"

-Matthew 22:37

The next verse pays so many premiums on this commandment by saying *"this is the first and great commandment"*(Matthew 22:38).

This form of adultery is like adding impurities to pure water. The misery in this is that, once an impurity is introduced into pure water, it changes all the properties of the water, most especially, its freezing point and boiling point.

In the same vein, once a service made unto God is being adulterated, it becomes so difficult to seek His face. This adulteration hinders a form of intimacy with God, which allows you to relate with God as one, just as He [God] has made marriage and intimacy as one.

Jesus reminds us just how deadly this form of adultery can be, when He said;

"No one can serve two masters. Either you will hate one and love the other, or you will be devoted to one and despise the other"

-Matthew 6:24

It is important as believers that we leave the world behind us, the cross before us. No turning back.

Marital: This form of adultery often happens when couples begin to drift apart into their own separate worlds. It occurs when couples no longer spend quality time together.

The moment couples no longer have shared interests, activities or goals, then, marital adultery starts to set in. The lack of shared interests and activities creates a marital void which will be fulfilled by someone else outside the marriage.

"Do not deprive one another, except perhaps by agreement for a limited time, that you may devote yourselves to prayer; but then come together again, so that satan may not tempt you because of your lack of self-control."

-1 Corinthians 7:5

The couple must always have a "point of agreement" in their discussion, deliberation, suggestion or argument or else, the devil will hijack the moment of conflicting interest in the home and use it to his advantage by causing the couples to stay away from each other. Hence, they fall victim of marital adultery.

Mental: There is no way we can talk about physical adultery without talking about mental adultery. It is one of the biggest problems destroying marriages today.

Mental adultery is to look with an intentional and conscious desire to gratify lust; to picture situations in the mind; to think adultery in the mind with a person to the point that if the opportunity were presented you would commit the physical act.

Mental adultery also took place during Biblical times. The Bible mentions this form of adultery several times, particularly in Matthew and Mark. Jesus said;

"But I say unto you, that whosoever looks on a woman to lust after her hath committed adultery with her already in his heart"

-Matthew 5:28

"Out of the heart of a man proceed evil thoughts, adulteries, fornications,"

-Mark 7:20-21

What's so sabotaging about this form of adultery is the fact that people don't take it as seriously because no physical act has taken place.

However, inappropriate thoughts, visualizing about a person other than your partner, fantasizing about other people as you're sleeping with your partner, visiting certain places knowing that a person you're sexually attracted to will be there, seeking eye contact with someone you're sexually attracted to, watching pornography, especially if your partner doesn't know about it and looking at different social media profiles of people that you have sexual interest in, among other things. While this form of infidelity may seem harmless, it will silently sabotage your relationship.

Dire Consequences of Adultery (After adultery nothing remains the same again)

"He who commits adultery lacks sense; he who does it destroys himself."

-Proverbs 6:32

1. **Loss of trust and confidence among couples:**

Trust creates good ambience in marriage. It enables dependability and reliability in marriage. Therefore, when this trust is destroyed through adultery, couples begin to relate together in fear.

When there is lack of trust between two couples, they begin to do things separately, conflict of interest set in, rift, suspecting one another, crisis in the family and so on.

Also, when children discover that their Mom or Dad has been unfaithful, they may feel insecure in the relationship and suffer a loss of trust in the cheating partner. This is true even if you don't tell the kids that a parent is cheating, because they'll feel the tension that exists between them. If one of you walks out of the relationship, your children may feel responsible for the split, regardless of how often you tell them that the responsibility lies with the parents.

2. **Loss of honor, respect and worth in the home and society:**

"For by means of a whorish woman a man is brought to a piece of bread"

-Proverbs 6:26a.

Whenever a man commits adultery, no matter how highly placed he is, he's brought down.

Once upon a time, a university lecturer, professor and highly respected personnel committed adultery with a student in his school. When he was caught, he was embarrassed that his fifth generation will still not be able to withstand the stigma.

Every individual enjoys the feeling of being a king with a divinely decorated crown, but adultery takes the crown off of the head of the fellow who commits it.

Take for instance; as highly placed as David was when he committed adultery, people began to throw stones at him. What a loss of honor and respect? A whole king! Jezebel, a first-class queen was fed on by dogs just because of this same adultery.

Assuming Joseph had slept with Potiphar's wife, he would definitely have been killed (according to the law of Egypt at that time). His master would have been highly disappointed in him (being a vessel of God).

Thank God for his grace upon Joseph. Also Parents are supposed to provide appropriate role models to children, but cheating isn't something you want to teach your kids. Many adult children whose parents were unfaithful lost their respect and honor for their parents and they are likely to repeat this cycle. Extended family might take sides against the cheating spouse or become embroiled in the relationship. The reputation of your family would suffer loss.

3. **Physical and mental pollution:**

Pollution is the act of contaminating or bringing something to undesirable state by introducing harmful substances.

The harmful substance here is adultery. In the process of sleeping with a strange woman/man, the blood is being polluted. Some diseases like HIV/AIDS, gonorrhea, herpes, syphilis, etc., are transmitted during the intercourse, it does not matter how highly anointed you may be.

A lot of diseases that now dominate some families today were not foundational, but at a particular point in time, they were introduced into the family through adultery. The use of condom does not totally prevent the transmission of physical diseases, let alone the spiritual ones.

Adultery also leads to mental pollution because there is always a sense of regret after it's been committed. The mind is always in trouble because there are many uncertainties that could occur after the act.

The counterfeit pleasure of an affair can never overcome the way Infidelity can destroy a life and marriage.

A spouse who is caught up in adultery is living only for the moment, caught up in a fantasy of excitement and desire, and ignoring the very real consequences. Infidelity can destroy a life and marriage.

4. Spiritual detachment and erroneous union:

"Stolen waters are sweet, and bread eaten in secret is pleasant"

-Proverbs 9:17

Some people know the secret of being one with God. Hence, they try to defile this oneness by making themselves channels through which you would sin against God.

Adultery is defilement against yourself, betrayal of your trust with your partner and most especially, it is a sin against God.

The truth is, adultery takes you far from God to be one with the devil. This is a dangerous union because the devil has nothing to give.

Your relationship with God will suffer from a break in fellowship. It will experience God's discipline.

5. Separation from communion with the Holy Spirit

Automatically, when a man becomes one with the devil, there's a great separation between him and the Holy Spirit of God. Some people will say once you are born again, even if you commit adultery, the Holy Spirit will not leave you. If the Holy Spirit does not want to leave you, by the time he deals with you, you'd look for a way to run away from Him deliberately.

Though He [God] is merciful, he can come to your aid if you're ready to repent and forsake your sins. The water that serves as comfort for fishes today, will also serve as a cooking medium for it when it dies. Despite that we live in the era of grace, if you now feel covered by grace to commit adultery; don't forget that the same grace will bury you when you die into adultery (Romans 6:1).

Thank God for people like David who know the importance of communion with Holy Spirit, and that's why he cried out loudly "take not thy Spirit from me" (Psalm 51:11). Some might conclude that all Christians are hypocrites. Leadership among those you have led in the past might also be diminished in impact.

6. Exit from life of favor and grace to death, judgment and Condemnation

"Behold, I will throw her onto a sick-bed, and those who commit adultery with her I will throw into great tribulation, unless they repent of their works."

-Revelation 2:22

People often believe they don't die immediately after committing adultery. The truth is, people fail to remember that the human body dies gradually.

Physical death doesn't occur suddenly as many people think it to be, but gradually. This also applies to spiritual death.

Assuredly, grace and favor accompanies anyone who loves God and does His will. However, for an adulterer or adulteress, the reverse might likely be the case because God detest every act of disobedience as much as He loves you.

1. Generational pollution. Your part at conception of a child through adultery might trigger an abortion, the killing of an innocent child. This same sin might be visited upon the family for four generations.

One of the things you need to be careful about is the generation that will be coming through you and after you. God pronounced adverse judgment on Judah. This judgment raged up to tenth generations which was Jesse.

However, the adverse judgment only stopped on David, which happened to be the eleventh generation.

Sometime ago, a young man impregnated a girl. Since it was unwanted, they went for abortion. However, because the abortion wasn't done perfectly; the lady began to feel pains after a month. The young man could not stand the pains, so he ran away.

After some time, the pains kept multiplying and no one was there to help. She eventually died. But, before she died, she made an evil pronouncement on the young man and his generations yet unborn. Till today, the generation of that young man always loses their first child. What a generational pollution!

*"Because she took her whoredom lightly, **she polluted the land,** committing adultery with stone and tree."*

Jeremiah 3:9

Seven (7) ways by which the Seed of Adultery is planted and How to uproot them

- By sight

  "They have eyes full of adultery, insatiable for sin. They entice unsteady souls. They have hearts trained in greed. Accursed children!

  -2Peter 2:14

- By spouse neglect. Lack of balance in married life with failure to attend to romantic aspect of marriage, the marital friendship and sexual intimacy/betrothed love.

- By wrong association. Close friendships with others who have divorced or been unfaithful. Withdraw from such friendship to save your marriage.

- By unresolved past issues and relationships. Previous infidelity. You can seek counsel from a marriage counselor.
- By a love for pleasure

  "When I fed them to the full, they committed adultery and trooped to the houses of whores."

  -Jeremiah 5:7
- By spiritual attacks. Pray against such an attack.
- By a desire to punish, exert dominance or display ego. Strong resentment and anger meant for a father, mother or significant other that is mis-directed at the spouse.

In conclusion, your marriage can only be as secured as your togetherness always. Never give the devil the slightest break between you and your partner or else, he will make a mess out of your marriage. Your home remains guarded as long as both partners are together in the marriage covenant of God.

SPIRITUAL NUGGET 5

Never give the devil the slightest break between you and your partner or else, he will make a mess out of your marriage. Your home remains guarded as long as both partners are together in the marriage covenant of God.

SEEDS OF DEFILEMENT

PART TWO
SEEDS OF CONFLICT

"For the Word of God is living and powerful and sharper than any two-edged sword, piercing even to the dividing apart of soul and spirit, and of the joints and marrow, and is a discerner of the thoughts and intents of the heart"

-HEBREW 4:12

"For your maker is your husband, the Lord of hosts is His name; and your Redeemer is the Holy One of Israel; He is called the God of the whole earth

ISAIAH 54:5

CHAPTER SIX
THE SEED OF JEALOUSY

We all have the desire to guard and protect something or someone we care for, with every available means. This is the kind of jealousy God feels for His own. A caring father corrects and chastens his child when he does wrong or persists in an activity that is dangerous, because parents want the best for their children. So does God.

This chapter will open the eyes of your understanding to the meaning of jealousy, the source of jealousy, differences between jealousy and envy with Biblical references. Also, emphasis will be made on the kinds or types of jealousy, root or causes of jealousy, effects and ways of overcoming the seed of jealousy or turning the ungodly jealousy to a Godly one.

MEANING OF JEALOUSY

The word *Jealous* in Hebrew is "qana" which means to be zealous. To be jealous is to be vigilant in maintaining or protecting something within our jurisdiction. In other words, it also means to be passionately providing, protecting, polishing and promoting onto God's perfect desire and design. In the Biblical days, we saw how God was fiercely protective of the Israelites who worshipped Him and by extension He is fiercely protective of those who live righteously, doing good works, being loving, honest, living with integrity, caring for those in need living and seeking peace with other people.

DIFFERENCES BETWEEN JEALOUSY AND ENVY

Here, I will exclusively talk about the differences between Jealousy and envy. Jealousy is not similar to envy as people think, in fact, they are opposites. JEALOUSY simply means to zealously guide and protect what you have in order not to lose or misplace it. It is a defensive reaction to a perceived threat in a valued relationship. It is an intensive desire for something that belongs to you while ENVY is excessive desire for things that belong to others. It is carnal and destructive. The source of Envy is satan. He was clamoring to be like God. He envied the position of God. He wasn't satisfied with where he was placed.

The story of the two harlots in 1 King 3: 16 give more insight to the differences between Jealousy and Envy. The woman that lost her child was envious of the biological mother of the child. She was coveting or desiring that the child should be killed while the biological mother was defending and passionately protecting what belonged to her, which is jealousy. "Everyone experiences jealousy at some point, no matter how saintly they are"

SOURCE OF JEALOUSY

In Deuteronomy 4, God makes a staggering declaration of His nature and character by describing himself as a "Jealous God" who is a consuming fire. Also in Exodus 34, God declares that 'Jealous' is one of His names. It is interesting to know that all through the Bible from Genesis to Revelation, God always draws His people's attention to Himself and when their attention wanders from him, He is quick to draw them back. This attribute of God is known as jealousy. Therefore, it is glaring to say that the source of jealousy is God and the source of envy is satan.

TYPES OF JEALOUSY

I will give succinct explanation on the types of jealousy in this section.

There are two main types of jealousy;

- Godly or Positive Jealousy (2 Corinthians 11: 2) and
- Ungodly or negative jealousy (Song 8:6)

Godly Jealousy or righteous Jealousy

Godly jealousy is in the dimension of God's jealousy towards his people. God would not just allow anything or anyone to damage what He has made. God is one with us in fellowship and He will be jealous about that oneness because intimacy and communion with God is like a marriage situation that provokes God to jealousy.

"For thy maker is thine husband, the lord of hosts is his name and their redeemer the Holy one of Israel; the God of the whole world shall he be called"

Isaiah 54:5

Jealousy is not a capricious mood with God. It is the ultimate expression of His being. In His infinite holiness, God is supremely dedicated to preserving His honor with exclusive devotion and worship. No dedicated husband or wife having integrity would want to share their spouse with a substitute – neither does God.

God expects our exclusive devotion. When we give preference to anything instead of Him, it is idolatry. God is zealous for His Holiness. Both in His wrath and love, God always remains the same. God's jealousy is not associated or motivated by insecurity, anxiety, frustration, self – centeredness, or pride as it's often the case with man's jealousy. The jealousy of a Holy God is the essence of His moral character, confidence on the part of people and ground for fear on the part of His enemies.

The divine and natural matrimony are the only excuses for jealousy. Husband and wife should try to keep infidelity aside. Adultery is not allowed. When jealousy is in place the next response is attack. Whenever God realized that the Israelites were adulterating, He attacked them for what they had done and when He eventually found repentance in them, He attacked those that oppressed them. Jealousy expresses oneness with the possession.

Ungodly jealousy

Ungodly jealousy is when you are jealous over the wrong things. For instance, jealousy among men with their material resources could be said to be ungodly. The Bible says that the love of money is the beginning of all evil. Jealousy between man and any material thing is destruction. Whatever will make a man become one with any material property has made that man lose his place in decency, dignity and integrity. In fact, that is even idolatry as far as God is concerned. Whatever you love more than God becomes idolatry.

"You are provoking God to Jealousy by becoming jealous about something."

The relationship between us and God should be reciprocal of Jealousy.

God tested Abraham on the platform of jealousy and He passed. That is, God is Jealous of you and you will also be Jealous about your relationship with God. The Bible says that you should guard your heart for out of it, springs the issues of life (Proverbs 4:23). Guarding your relationship with God jealously is very critical because it means that you are to guard it with all sense of humility, alertness, vigilance and even in suspicion.

"Therefore, let him that thinks he stands take heed lest he fall'.

1 Corinthians 10:11

Guard your stand in Christ with jealousy. Be suspicious about it. Examine yourself. Stay committed to the teachings of Christ and His commandments as a proof of your allegiance to Him. This will make you become connected in a way that keeps your jealousy for Christ and everything associated with Him.

Whatever you have which God cannot intercept is Human jealousy.

Jesus Christ sent his disciple to release the horse and told them if they ask them who needs it, just by mentioning His name, they would release it. What do you have that at the mention of Christ you cannot release? What do you have that God cannot intercept? What do you have that looks so difficult for you to let go?

We must understand that everything in our custody today is really not our own, it all belongs to God. He just entrusted it to you as a caretaker, (Psalm 24:1-2). So, expressing human jealousy towards material things can actually be dangerous to you as a person and everyone around you. No one can receive anything except it is given from above, (John3:27). Therefore, with this mentality you should maintain a right perspective of jealousy- the God kind.

What could we possibly have in our life that arouses God's jealousy? Is it beneficial to have a personal relationship with a jealous God?

Truthfully, having a relationship with God is what gives us true security. By doing this He becomes our defense against every adversary. Therefore, God requires our total reliance on Him, so, making any other thing stand in the way of our total dependence on Him attracts His wrath on us. We can liken this to what the Bible says in Deuteronomy 22:9 which forbid anyone from planting different kinds of seed on their vine yard to avoid defilement.

"You shall not sow your vineyard with different kinds of seeds, lest the fruit of your seed which you have sown and the fruit of your vineyard be defiled"

-Deuteronomy 22:9

The above scripture reveals that trying to attach anything with God is defilement.

Therefore, we will briefly look into areas that we have to be jealous of in our dealings with God, in order to maintain our devotion and commitment to Him, which are:

Our Time - *"There is a season for everything, and a time for every event under heaven"*(Ecclesiastes 3:1). We have no control over eternity, or even the hectic demands of a single day, but God assures us that He is looking out for our best interests. He wants us to take time to be continually renewed physically and spiritually (Exodus 20:9-11; Matthew 11:28-30). As we give more time to God, our level of devotion and trust strengthens our divine relationship with Him. As a result, we should spend time in prayer, in the study of His word, and in consistent fellowship, this will make our lives pleasing to Him always. Failure to do this will cause us to replace Godly jealousy with ungodly jealousy.

Our Possessions- "You see, heaven–even the highest heavens–belongs to the LORD, along with the earth and all that is in it" (Deuteronomy 10:14). Thinking we own our possessions cultivates pride, selfishness, and ingratitude. But when we seek Him, God supplies all our needs [food, finances, clothing] because He is faithful in all His promises (Matthew 6:33; Philippians 4:19). God created all things, and He never transferred ownership to His people. We are, however, expected to be faithful and wise managers of all that God has entrusted in our care. God rewards faithfulness in caring for our families and finances (Luke 16:10-13).

Our Purpose – "...You must love the Lord your God with all your heart, with all your soul, and with your entire mind'" (Matthew 22:37). God is concerned with the whole person. If we are broken-hearted, He heals our heartaches and binds up our wounds. When our enemies attack us, God becomes our rock and fortress in whom our soul finds rest and hope. Even if fear and worry threatens to consume us, God hears our prayers and guards our hearts and minds through Christ Jesus with His supernatural peace. The essence of our creation is to glorify God (Isaiah43:21). Therefore, fulfilling our purpose guarantees total security from God, He becomes jealous over us.

ILLUSTRATIONS OF PEOPLE THAT WERE JEALOUS

1. The foolish man was jealous of his property or wealth (Luke 12:16-21)
2. Saul and his throne. He was jealous of his throne to the point of killing anyone trying to take it away from him. The jealousy later turned to envy.
2. King Herod and the Killing of male babies under two years old. There was a massacre because of his throne (Matthew 2:16)
3. Apostle Paul knew that the Corinthians' faithfulness to the one true God was threatened by the prevalence of sin in their society and by the influence of false teachers. He spoke to the Corinthian members as a father would do to a daughter he loved and wanted to protect, because he loved them in that same way. He was on guard for them.

ROOT OF UNGODLY JEALOUSY

1. Perceiving a threat to what you have and you don't want to lose.
2. Sense of Insecurity.
3. Hardships and heartache in one's life and family
4. Blindness to truth
5. Fear
6. Obsession
7. Pride

8. Lack of trust
9. Selfishness, covet etc.

EFFECTS OF UNGODLY JEALOUSY

Here, we will talk about the effects of ungodly jealousy so that we can understand how grave its consequences could be and by this we will be able to take preventive measures against any little rise of jealousy. These are:

It leads to oneness.

Oneness means becoming one with something or someone. You are not to become one with anything; you are to become one with two things. God and man (Your husband or wife).

These are the oneness that is permissible. Any oneness outside these two is an adulteration. It is Corruption. It will corrupt that person. satan became one with what he had.

Another danger of becoming one with materialism is that it doesn't satisfy. It will always create a space and that hole will be from jealousy. It will not be enough. You will be thinking it will be finished. There is nothing that you become one with that will ever be enough. There is only one sufficiency which is God.

"Any sufficiency you create outside God becomes Jealousy"

The more you become one with something, the more devastating the experience will be. Notice what happened to Jacob. He became one with Rachel and transferred that oneness to Joseph. So, when he lost him, he was nothing. Jacob was an inventor, adventurer and achiever but for a window period that Joseph was not around, he was nothing. There was no achievement recorded to his name. Technically, he was dead because he had become one with Joseph. He began to bleed incessantly until he saw Joseph. In fact, when he was told that Joseph was still alive, he said "Let me see him and die (Genesis 45:26-28). Why? It was because he was a living dead.

Also, Jonathan and David were so attached or knitted together as one. But if you notice, it didn't affect David. It affected Jonathan only. David's heart was always with the Lord, that was why God called him; a man after his own heart.

Not that he was double minded with Jonathan but he put the relationship in perspective. You can be very close to people and technically become one with them yet it will still be in perspective.

Any oneness or strange oneness would drop a seed of jealousy.

Any strange oneness or attachment with someone or something will become an idol which is a sin before God. Take for instance, the incident that occurred between Lot's wife at Sodom and Gomorrah. There was oneness in that place.

It is possible that Lot's wife was the one that negotiated or put pressure on her husband to put away with Abraham, so that they could go and settle there.

Although, we did not hear much about lot's wife but when you hear something about somebody and the thing that struck your mind is disaster, my dear, the disaster started long ago. It is a gradual process. Lot's wife became one with Sodom and Gomorrah. She became one with Baal and the end was destructive.

Some people are into bad relationships because of Jealousy but they would rather die in that wrong relationship than to leave and go somewhere else. They have become one with it.

Some people have become jealous of their work. They have become one with it. If they are sacked or lose the job, they became miserable and can even commit suicide because they don't see light outside it again.

Some people are jealous of their influence. If John the Baptist was jealous of his influence, he wouldn't have pointed to Jesus or transferred the glory or the influence to him. He was a worthy caretaker. He was the first person that came to limelight with the word of God. Yet, he recognized His role and maintained it. In fact his ministry was reducing but he preferred to be decreasing while Christ was increasing (John 3:30-31). Whatever you have become oneness with, either work, education, relationship, even position or title, you must surrender them to God.

Another effect of ungodly jealousy is that "**It will bring harm to ourselves, our families, and, worst of all, it will destroy our souls.**

When we engage in ungodly jealousy we shift our trust from God to things that will expose us to danger and make us vulnerable to the attacks of the evil one

WAYS OF OVERCOMING UNGODLY JEALOUSLY

1. **Trust God and Your spouse**

Trust is a vital means to overcome jealousy; you must trust God to provide everything you need in life because He has promised that He will never leave nor forsake you.

2. **Have faith**

Faith is a supernatural force that births every notable walk and work with God, you cannot please God without having faith in Him, it was the Faith that Abraham had in God that made him become the father of nations. Your faith can launch you into deep realms of exploits.

3. **Be prayerful and study the word of God**

Prayer is a powerful force that can combat any unruly act; also the word of God is sharper than any two edged sword.

"For the Word of God is living and powerful and sharper than any two-edged sword, piercing even to the dividing apart of soul and spirit, and of the joints and marrow, and is a discerner of the thoughts and intents of the heart"

-Hebrew 4:12

Therefore by being prayerful and placing our confidence in God's word we will be strengthened against jealousy.

4. **Be truthful**

Jesus Christ said that the truth you know will make you free. Whenever you walk in the truth you will never be defeated because the truth always liberates.

5. **Stop comparison**

Never compare yourself to anyone, run your own race with your eyes looking straight before you for the Bible *says "...but they measuring themselves by themselves, and comparing themselves among themselves, are not wise"* (2 Corinthians 10:12).

6. **Have Abundance Mentality**

As you think in your heart so you will become, if you think abundance you will see abundance but if you think otherwise you will experience insufficiency and this will in turn make you insecure. Therefore, always have abundance mentality so that jealousy will not take any root in you.

God should be our sufficiency in life nothing else can take His place. But, we have to be intentional in our devotion and commitment to Him.

We must avoid the seed of jealousy that has been discussed in this chapter.

SPIRITUAL NUGGET 6

There is only one sufficiency which is God. Any sufficiency you create outside God becomes Jealousy.

"Pride goes before destruction, a haughty spirit before a fall"

-PROVERBS 16:18

CHAPTER SEVEN
THE SEED OF PRIDE

"Pride goes before a fall and a haughty spirit before destruction"

-Proverb 16:18

It is amazing that you have read this book with understanding so far. Now we have come to a very subtle and seemingly harmless but defiling trait among humans today: the seed of pride.

This chapter will help you discover that pride could be such a destructive force. Pride is a seed that defiles the soul and spirit. Unfortunately, pride has become part of the day-to-day experience among people at every level of human relationship. Some people don't worry about attitudes and actions that are aimed at vain glory, self-promotion and ego.

A right perception on pride

"Blow your trumpet; only truthfully and humbly"

-Anonymous

We need to make some clarifications here. Many have the wrong idea about the concept of pride. Actually, pride can be a positive and negative influence. Bob can be *proud* of the brilliance of his daughter, Jane, in High school. That doesn't make him a proud man. A positive appreciation of other's efforts and achievements that is devoid of conceits, aggrandizement or lust for fame is a *good pride.*

You can blow your trumpet and have *pride* in your achievements, but not with the minutest toga of self-centeredness and crave for fame. Trying to impress others will lead you to being negatively proud but trying to impress God will make you grow in humility. When you blow your trumpet with a false or fake sense of worth, you are arrogantly proud.

So, what is pride?

Here is a common definition of pride:

"A feeling of deep pleasure or satisfaction in an achievement, an accomplishment or in someone else or something else but it's also been described as conceit, egotism, vanity, vainglory, all over one's own appearance or status in life and not just something that's been accomplished. It is an inwardly directed emotion that can easily offend others and carries with it a connotation that displays an inflated sense of one's own worth or personal status and typically makes one feel a sense of superiority over others and can easily make someone look condescendingly at others".

-Jack Wellman

I cannot agree less! Notice words such as conceit, vainglory, vanity, egotism and inflated sense, superiority in this definition. These are the elements of arrogant pride.

Pride is the inordinate exaltation and glorification of oneself above others and beyond proportion. Pride is the direct opposite of humility, piety and self-effacement. The proud looks down on all others and he always has the *superior arguments, the better disposition, the most effective method, the best possession and the greater strength.* No one else has.

Those who manifest pride are its victims. When pride takes over a willing heart, all that is left is a disposition that portrays a sense of 'no one else matters except me'. It is a stranglehold from which a victim needs liberation.

History is replete with names of people like Hitler who subdued people with arrogant pride and ended up in prideful suicide when it became apparent that his ambition of conquering Europe was only a mirage.

The Bible also bears record of people like King Saul who refused to be humble and meek, but later had to be brought low, humiliated and struck down by his pride. He refused to acknowledge his sin. An Un-repentant heart is a prideful heart.

There is no basis for vanity and pride

"..... A man can receive nothing, except it be given him from heaven"

-John 3:27

Do you sometimes wonder why some people lack what others have in abundance? Natural endowments and innate abilities; health and wealth; fame and favor and comparative advantages are just opportunities, sometimes unmerited. If it were possible to determine how to be born, no one will be born poor! I am sure every child would choose stupendously rich parents over the poor. However, how and where you are born are decisions you cannot make. It is simply a happen stance.

When you fail to recognize that you cannot influence your birth, you will become proud of your attainments in life. It is wise to understand that life and times are divinely orchestrated privileges and opportunities

"For I say, through the grace given unto me, to every man that is among you, not to think of himself more highly than he ought to think; but to think soberly, according as God has dealt to every man the measure of faith"

Romans 12:3

So what is the basis for pride? None because God gives everyone as He deem fit.

The origin and the spread of the seed of pride

Among God's arch angels was the "son of the morning", the resplendent Lucifer. He was the originator of the seed of pride. It was identified as iniquity that was lodged within the originally perfect being. This was his defilement; it became his downfall.

"Thou was perfect in thy ways from the day that thou was created, till iniquity was found in thee"

-Ezekiel 28:15

Now let's talk about Adam. If you study Genesis Chapter 3, where Adam and Eve listened to the voice of rebellion and ate fruit from the forbidden tree. You will notice that, Adam never owned up to his disobedience to God's instruction not to eat of the fruit of the tree in the midst of Eden. He never did. The same seed of pride in satan was transferred to Adam through disobedience. The seed of disobedience is borne out of pride.

How to recognize the manifestation of the seed of pride

Now, how do you know if you are proud? Pride has symptoms and these symptoms are often glossed over, sneaky and sometimes remain undetected. When you begin to see everything with your eyes alone, the seed has started to grow.

Jonathan Edward summarized the signs that one is proud in seven characteristic traits: defensiveness, harshness, superficiality, fault-finding, presumption, desperation for attention and neglect of others. Nothing can be farther from the truth.

Pride begins in the mind

Pride, can manifest as wrong, evil, inflated and pompous self-conversation at the thought level. Jesus said, *"Out of the abundance of the heart, the mouth speaks"*[Matthew 12:34].This implies that, before a prideful talk, attitude and action comes prideful thinking.

Like every other sinful practice, pride begins at the thought level.

Another instance of prideful thinking can occur when a younger or less opportune individual eventually begins to progress into a higher position of authority than yourself, and you feel nauseated by this so much that you begin to lust and wish that you had what they are getting and not them.

Words like, why him? Why not me? At least I'm far better and smarter! Gradually, you start getting heinous ideas against your neighbor.

God hates pride

If there is anything God hates so much, it is pride and idolatry. He hates this twin with profound passion. A proud man or woman ascribes the honor of creation and sustenance to them self. They speak and live as if they can survive without God and the contribution of other people.

Evidently, the proud equates him or herself with God! In Proverbs 8:13, King Solomon exclaimed *"the fear of the Lord is to hate evil: pride, and arrogancy, and the evil way, and the forward mouth* (which speaks proudly)*, do I hate"*

Interestingly, pride produces and is at the center of other vices that God equally hates.

"These six things does the Lord hates, yes, seven are an abomination to Him: A proud look, a lying tongue, and hands that shed innocent blood. An heart that devises wicked imaginations, feet that be swift in running to mischief, A false witness that speaks lies, and he that sows discord among brothers"

-Proverbs 6:16-19

Can you see how pride relates to other sins? When you become proud, you are, at the same time, committing at least six other sins which are bound to attract God's fury.

Again, pride does not allow you to ask God for help. It tells you that you have it all; know it all and can run it all.

Common Premise for Pride

Pride manifests itself in several areas. Let's see some of them with Biblical characters.

High Place and Position:

You can become proud when you find yourself on a higher pedestal than others. You may forget that, such place or position was not attained solely by your power, wisdom and influence alone. You did not arrive at that level without the help of God and people who contributed to your success directly or indirectly; so why have you become puffed up and bloated with the perks of such position and place that you relegate the creator and others to the background?

Herod

"And upon a set day Herod, arrayed in royal apparel, sat upon his throne, and made an oration unto them. And the people gave a shout, saying, it is the voice of a god, and not of man. And immediately the angel of the Lord smote him, because he gave not God the glory and was eaten of worms and gave up the ghost"

-Acts 12:21-23

When a man wants to take the place of God, he is sure to meet disaster. Unbridled consciousness of place and position makes you to relegate God, the giver of all opportunities, to a secondary being, subservient to you. Had Herod known this, he wouldn't have been eaten by worms!

Knowledge and intellect

Who gives wisdom? Who makes one person to be wiser or more knowledgeable than the other? How can anyone become wise without learning from those who have risen before him or her in wisdom?

The truth is knowledge puffs up, but love edifies. God is the source of all inspiration and knowledge. The power for oratory and eloquence; the gift of charisma and brilliance, and the ability to do things better than others are privileges from God for which no one should boast.

Possession, pace and progress

To be rich and prosperous is not a sin in itself. However, becoming proud about it is the problem. The masterpieces of today will soon become antiquity tomorrow. It is easier for the seed of pride to spring up in a rich man. That is why the Holy Scriptures says it is difficult for a rich man to enter into heaven, not that he cannot enter.

You need to bear in mind that, our patriarchs in the faith: Abraham, Isaac, Jacob, Job and King David were all rich and prosperous. However, they were men after God's own heart with all meekness and humility; they sought God and did not rely on vanity, riches and pride.

Listen to a young rich man in Jesus' parable,

"... he said, this will I do, I will pull down my barns, and build Greater; and there will I bestow all my fruits and my goods. And I will say to my soul, Soul, you have much goods laid up for many years, take your ease, eat, drink, and be merry"

-Luke 12:18, 19

Friend, when you plan as if God doesn't exist or like He has no say in your affairs, you are being controlled by subtle manifestations of the seed of pride. There was neither a single acknowledgment nor place for God in the plan of the rich young man. Unfortunately, his trust was in his money.

Pride of possession most times leads to idolatry. How? This happens because you literarily worship any possession that makes you proud.

Power and privileges

Like alcohol, power can get people intoxicated. Privileges can be abused. Power to control and dominate; direct and discipline as well as privilege to determine the fate of others are susceptible to manifestation of pride. Except you see political, economic, religious or social power and privileges as a test of character, you are bound to abuse them.

Remember Nebuchadnezzar? His pride about lofty position brought him down from the pinnacle of power and glory to a grazing beast. Hear him,

"... is not this great Babylon, that I have built for the kingdom by the might of my power, and for the honor of my majesty?"

-Daniel 4:30

Proud people don't learn fast neither do they see the need to make amends. Belshazzar, his son, would not learn from the evil of what pride did to his father. In his proud state, he desecrated the vessels of the house of God and had to pay dearly for it.

"But when his heart was lifted up, and his mind hardened in pride, he was deposed from his kingly throne, and they took his glory from him... "And you his son, O Belshazzar, have not humbled your heart, though you knew all this"

-Daniel 5:20.22

The outcome was that, His kingdom was not only divided, he died for his pride.

Race, age and face (Beauty)

Are some races destined to be impoverished while others must excel? Does age really matter when it comes to fulfillment and pleasing God? I don't think so. Is beauty the ultimate goal? Not at all! These are just privileges. When you become too conscious of your race, age and beauty, you may be tempted to be lifted up with pride. Remember the scriptures say *beauty is vain* (Proverbs 31:30).

Religion and worship

One of the major factors hindering the world's peace is religion. The cloak of religion has become a tool of pride even in Christianity. Today, among churches and other places of worship there is tension and contention for superiority. Many people who belong to a denomination, class, center of worship and religious belief see themselves as better or even 'holier' than others. Many have forgotten that Christianity goes beyond religion or worship. They fail to see it as a spiritual relationship with God that is cultivated in humility.

The '*holier than thou'* attitude is gradually destroying the fabrics of true Christianity. Many, nowadays, worship church founders and religious leaders because they feel such leaders are better than others. In the heart of many worshippers, the God of true religion is relegated behind the pomp of pride.

Have you not seen pomposity among so called '*men of God*'?

What else could be more popular in the Bible than divine anger and judgment against pride? The point is, God sees pride as heinous and devilish. Christians must also see it as so. Pride warps your view of the reality. You only see things from your own perspective and judgment.

DANGERS OF PRIDE

Pride puts a man under unnecessary tension

A proud individual is overly sensitive to what people say or think of him. Therefore, he or she becomes easily worn out and stressed out in the race for superiority; quest for excess attention and desire to receive praise.

Pride removes a man from the reach of grace

A typical example was the Pharisee who found it difficult to accept the free gift of grace and salvation by faith in Jesus who they knew to be a common son of a carpenter. Due to their societal status and religious knowledge and position; it was difficult to submit to the Grace and Truth about Jesus Christ. This attitude detached them from the grace of God that Jesus freely offered. Instead, they stuck to the law or better said-Hypocrisy!

Furthermore, a proud man or woman would rarely accept help, opportunities and free gifts as they believe they know what they want and can get it without anyone's help. So, they go through hell on earth and go to hell after death, just because they neither acknowledged man nor God and this act triggers God to show His superiority to them in a terrifying manner, for it is written;

"Every one that is proud in heart is an abomination to the Lord, through hand joined in hand, he shall not be unpunished"

-Proverbs 16:5

Shame

"When pride comes, then comes shame, but with the lowly is wisdom".

Proverbs 11:2

When you are proud, you easily tell lies. A proud man is put to shame when his claims turn out to be untrue. This shame can be personal or public.

Foolishness

As harsh as it may appear, a proud man is a fool. Think of it; is it not foolishness to put one's self on a cliff risking a great fall? That is where a proud man is.

"In the mouth of the foolish is a rod of pride: but the lips of the wise shall preserve them"

-Proverbs 14:3

Death

Pride can kill. A proud man will not want to seek medical help when he is sick. He knows the solution to it. Saul, the first king of Israel would probably not have died prematurely if he had sought for solution through the right channel in humility. But, in his pride, he resorted to the witch at Endor. A proud man dies foolishly because he would neither seek for nor accept counsel.

Fall

It is not bad to fall and rise up, but the proud falls and remains fallen because he has no humility to ask for help

How to root out the seed of pride

Friend, as you get closer to the end of this chapter, I cannot but advise, frankly, that you need to check out your life in the mirror of God's word. As evil as pride is, it is often difficult to spot by a proud person and if its opposite the case, he/she may not see himself as proud. But you must take definite steps to uproot the seed from your total being.

As you can see, pride separates us from God and limits our fellowship with God's people, so why choose to remain in pride? It is time for you to deliver yourself from the spirit of pride and get reconciled with God.

Swift mind-shift and repentance is crucial

There is no two-way to it: Pride is sin and the proud must own up and repent. Attempts to defend our haughty moves before the all-knowing God will only take us farther away from Him. He demands total repentance.

Moreover, since pride begins from the mind; it is important that you promptly detect and eliminate pride in your thought pattern. A prideful self-conversation must be detected and stopped promptly before the seed settles, germinates and bears fruits of destruction.

The way up is down

"Humble yourselves in the sight of the Lord, and He shall lift you up"

James 4:10

God sees differently from man. While man sees pride as the only way out of his inferiority complex; God sees the proud as a transgressor. To be high in God's rating, you need to humble yourself before Him. To be lifted up, He is passionately looking for sincere humility in you. The way up, is actually down.

SPIRITUAL NUGGET 7

Those who manifest pride are its victims. When pride takes over a willing heart all that is left is a disposition that portrays a sense of 'no one else matters except 'me'. It is a stronghold from which a victim needs liberation.

"Do not hasten in your spirit to be angry, for anger rests in the bosom of fools"

ECCLESIASTES 7:9

CHAPTER EIGHT
THE SEED OF ANGER

"Be not hasty in thy spirit to be angry: for anger rests in the bosom of fools".

-Ecclesiastes 7:9

Welcome to another wonderful chapter in this book. Remember that, your heart can be likened to a field which grows whatever seed that has been planted. Indeed, the human heart does not discriminate. It will grow whatever is planted and nurtured in it. This is why; you cannot permit good and evil seeds to be planted, nurture and bear fruit together in your heart. Trust me, the outcome is always disastrous.

Virtually everyone has experienced and expressed anger at one point or the other but what matters the most is what you do with the feeling. Anger is felt and expressed by different people in diverse ways.

For some, anger is expressed by yelling, screaming, hitting things or people while some other people simply simmer within and endure headaches, profuse sweating, dizziness, hot neck, belly aches and trembling. So pathetic!

satan wants to keep people bound to uncontrollable and harmful anger. He does this by consistently spreading the seeds of rage over their heart through diverse situations and under many circumstances.

Unfortunately, anger is a terrible slave master and a wild beast. It doesn't like to give up its prey easily. It seeks to drive its victims to unrestrained actions and reactions. We all need to be free from it.

I want to ask you: Do you over-react to provocations? Are you tired of hurting within and being oppressive to others? Do you feel dominated by a force and a rage you don't understand? Are you afraid of coming down with health issues like a nervous break-down, cardiovascular disease and more because of anger? Then help is here! Keep reading, and you will find liberty and freedom from the clutches of negative anger!

You wonder why I qualified the Anger I'm about to talk about? Yes, I mean "Negative Anger." Indeed, there is "Positive anger." It will be adequately explained in the later part of this chapter. However, you need to understand that, anger is like the explosion that takes place inside a car engine which produces the power that propels the car. When the explosion is under control, it will take the car to its destination but if not properly controlled it will both destroy the car and whoever is inside or around it.

SO, WHAT'S THE BIG DEAL ABOUT ANGER?

The Bible contains the word of God which can heal and restore the human spirit, soul and body. This is why I'm going to approach the concept of Anger from the scriptural perspective. When the Bible uses the word "anger"; its root meaning is found in the Greek word "orgizo" which means to make annoyed, provoke to rage or to irritate.

So, anger is expressed in feelings of irritation or displeasure towards an unwanted action from another person which is perceived to be disrespectful, threatening or neglectful. It comes from the failure of people to meet a significant standard or expectation. It short circuits' relationships and genuine satisfaction in life.

Don't get confused, not all kinds of anger are the same...

"in your anger do not sin" do not let the sun goes down while you are still angry."

-Ephesians 4:26

First, do you realize that God is infinitely righteous, loving and compassionate yet he can get angry? Oh! Step out of the cloud! Love can be expressed in anger. Take for instance, when you see someone or something trying to attack your child, how do you respond? Do you just sit there, smiling and wishing it would just disappear? I bet not! The first thing is the adrenaline pump that rouses you to top speed and radical actions to help your baby fend off that attack.

How much more than God? He will never give scorpions to His children who ask for fishes; instead, He will trample on snakes and scorpions on their behalf. Beat it! That needs a measure of ANGER!

There are several cases of anger in the Bible that we can use to classify anger into two major types based on what caused it and how it was expressed. They are namely; Positive or Righteous anger and Negative or Unrighteous anger.

Let's talk about Positive or Righteous Anger

"Therefore the LORD was very angry with Israel, and removed them out of his sight: there was none left but the tribe of Judah only."

-2Kings 17:18

This is the type of anger usually attributed to God in the scripture, and it is generally in response to sin and works of the devil.

Certain men and women of God in scriptures were also recorded to have displayed this type of Anger.

Meet King David, Apostle Paul, and Jesus Christ!

King David was a man after God's heart. His life was filled with wars, conflicts, victories and triumph. Trust me, this man of God was acquainted with righteous and positive anger.

At one time as a young shepherd boy, he demonstrated righteous anger when he saw Goliath, a robust, tall and powerful Philistine warrior who despicably mocked the people of Israel, challenging them and their God openly for 40 straight days. Wow!

No one could lift a finger; in fact, everyone including King Saul was hiding behind rocks and holes. Then, the unexpected happened when David, a controversial and remarkably courageous boy showed up on the battlefield.

The moment David heard about the dire situation, his response was... "Who is this uncircumcised Philistine...bragging before the people of God?" Now, he wasn't saying this like a sissy...he was ANGRY. He couldn't wait to get this enemy down! He felt like an insult to God's people was a reproach against God. He wasn't just going to sit behind rocks or hide in holes while this ugly situation persists. He was determined to do something about it. He was stirred up, he was furious, he was ready, he was ANGRY! If this does not make you angry, then what would?

Should it be trivial insults against your personality, a friend at the office who wouldn't return your pleasantries, your parking space that was rudely hijacked or just moodiness for no reason! Hey, Friend! Come off of all that pettiness and be aroused for the Kingdom of God, rise up for righteousness, rise up for dignity, rise up without reservation, rise up in strict discontent, rise up for swift action, rise up in Jesus Name! I challenge you to be POSITIVELY ANGRY!

Some pastors don't mind when satan takes out some of their members physically, spiritually and emotionally, they feel it's just the pressure of society;

there is nothing that can be done. I beg to differ. Pastor! Rise up for the Sheep that the Lord has put in your charge, you will account for each one of them! Don't give the enemy any more free time. The devil is a lying coward. Don't buy his antics and scary displays. Rise up against him. Stop passivity; take responsibility. Rise up in Jesus Name. BE RIGHTEOUSLY ANGRY!

Apostle Paul could not endure demonic praises from a young slave girl who had a spirit of divination when he walked the streets Macedonia. This girl would say, "These are the men sent from God to show the way of salvation." It sounded harmless, but it was from the enemy of the gospel and the salvation of men-satan! Paul became angry, and he commanded the unclean spirit to depart from the girl, and it was flung-out instantly. She was totally delivered (Acts 16:16-20). A clear message: God's praise will remain on the lips of His people and not familiar spirits.

Jesus Christ: He demonstrated righteous anger against Pharisees who didn't want him to heal on the Sabbath day because they thought it was unlawful to show love for the sick on such a Holy day (Mark 3:5).

He also showed righteous anger when he saw money changers buying and selling in the temple by throwing their goods away and chasing them out with a whip because of his passion for His father's house and sanity in among true worshippers (Mark 11: 15-17).

Now, what is an Unrighteous or Negative Anger?

"An angry man stirs up dissension, and a hot-tempered one commits many sins"

Proverbs 29:22

This is the type of anger that the Bible condemns because it defiles the person and can cause damage to lives and properties. It is motivated by personal discomfort, discontentment, and selfish desires. Anger becomes sinful when we begin to react against an offender instead of finding solutions to the problem.

Unrighteous anger also surfaces when things don't go the way we want them to go. A typical example of this anger is found in the Prophet Jonah. God directed him to go to Nineveh and preached the gospel.

However, it was disheartening to see Jonah rebelling against God's commandment to visit Nineveh. In the end, he was forced to finally preach the gospel, and the people of Nineveh repented. Prophet Jonah's plan didn't go as expected, so he became furious and disappointed. This man didn't expect God to easily forgive wicked Nineveh. Jonah couldn't grasp the wisdom in withdrawing wrath from such a godless people, not minding the fact that they have genuinely repented.

HERE ARE THE ROOTS OF ANGER

The next time you are angry, try to stop and ask yourself "why am I angry?" Anger always has a cause. There is always an underlying issue. Everyone has their own triggers for an angry response.

There are numerous ways through which anger sets in and dominates people's life. However, when we get angry, it is imperative to examine the cause and find the right thing to do to break-off its influence on our mind and emotions. Note that, whatever controls your emotions will influence your actions.

Anger can be rooted in Fear

Fear is an emotion that arises from an anticipation or awareness of danger. The greatest fear is the fear of death. However, there are other kinds of fear that stirs up defensiveness and self-preservation that is veiled by anger. So, whenever you find yourself angry just ask yourself "what am I afraid of?" Take off the veil!

Physical response to anger is identical to the way in which we respond to fear. Going by the manifestation of anger as earlier exposed in this chapter. Take for instance, when you find out that, you angrily shouted at a driver, who has attempted to cut you off in traffic. This reaction might be rooted in fear of the damage that could be done to your car by that reckless act. If you are angry at someone who made fun of you, then you might be afraid of losing people's respect or good impression about you.

In the Old Testament, King Saul was a typical example of someone whose fear led to uncontrollable, unrighteous, unnecessary and negative anger.

It began after David killed Goliath. As expected, women in the capital city were excited, so they came out and danced in the streets, as we read in 1 Samuel 18. Even more, they sang a provocative but straight forward song!

"As they danced, they sang: SAUL HAS SLAIN HIS THOUSAND AND

DAVID [HAS SLAINED] HIS TENS OF THOUSANDS,"

Funny! Did David really kill 10000? Well, Saul took this very seriously, even though it was not a big deal to David. To Saul, this was an INSULT! He became insecure and angry; more so, he became afraid of young David taking over the throne after his death instead of Jonathan His son. Worse still, he thought David might eventually rally support against his rule and overthrow it. He was so wrong, yet fear drove him to ceaseless episodes of rage, malice, and madness (1 Samuel 18: 7-12). FEAR is a powerful root of anger! Watch out!

Hurt:

When you perceive being rejected, unloved, mal-treated or unappreciated, you will often respond with anger. When Cain realized that his offering was not accepted in Genesis, he felt the emotional pain of rejection, and he responded in anger by killing his brother. Yes, he was hurt, offended and disappointed; yet did the murder of Abel change anything? Think about it!

Anger can be an upshot of past experiences

For most people, the past does not cease to show up in their present experiences. Therefore, if you were separated from the love and tender care of your parent from childhood due to one circumstance or the other, you might nurture anger towards anyone or people who played roles in this painful experience. When parents are divorced, their children typically experience anger, pain, isolation, and rejection.

Financial issues

Money plays a significant role in our day to day life. It is the soothing lubricant of our daily experiences. There is a sense of assurance and stability that comes with availability of funds. The lack of it means that you wouldn't be able to meet up with a lot of your needs which could then lead to the transfer of aggression. You may become easily irritated and fretful when you have needs without money to meet them.

Disappointment

Humans, no matter how well-meaning are limited in ability and resources. There are certain times when we are in positions where we expect certain things from individuals and they end up disappointing us. This has the tendency of making us angry at them and other people who might be linked with that situation.

A perfect example of this in the Bible was Naaman who was expecting Prophet Elijah to come out and pray for him, but to his uttermost dismay, he was told to go and wash in the Jordan River (2 King 5:11-12).

"But Naaman went away angry and said, I thought that he would surely come out to me and stand and call on the name of the Lord his God, wave his hand over the spot and cure me of my leprosy. 12 are not Abana and pharpar, the river in Damascus, better than any of the waters of Israel? Couldn't I washed in them and be cleansed? So, he turned and went off in a rage".

The reason behind his anger was because he expected Elisha to do one thing and Elisha did another. Watch out for pitfalls of unrealistic expectations.

CONSEQUENCES OF ANGER

"Anger is one letter short of danger."

-Eleanor Roosevelt

Anger is a gateway to so many problems, and it can cause significant damage not only in your life but in the lives of those around you. Anger is a defiler of the spirit, soul and body. When negative anger is conceived and left to grow, it eventually corrupts its victim in many ramifications. The following problems may arise as a result of uncontrolled anger.

Loneliness and separation

Negative anger separates us from fellowship with God and man. You cannot enjoy communion with the Holy Spirit while you are driven by carnal displeasure. The joy of the Lord has to be your strength and salvation.

More so, there is the tendency of hurting others in just a moment of an uncontrolled outburst. The more you hurt people, who care about you, the more they like to stay away from you. Don't be like a porcupine, and expect hugs from everyone. Certainly, they will stay away and you will be left alone. It's sad to be alone; deal with anger!

Destruction of property

When anger is not managed properly it can become rage, which leads to the damage of valuable items in the house or outside in public places. What an embarrassment! Avoid unnecessary grief, regret and loss- Deal with anger!

Health issues

Research has shown that protracted anger can lead to high blood pressure, heart problems, headaches, stomach-aches and digestive problems. So you have to deal with the seed of anger before it deals with you. You were meant to live a long and happy life. Deal with Anger!

Curse and demonic influences

When Jacob was saying his last words to his son, he pronounced a curse upon Simeon and Levi. He did so because of their anger which led them to kill several people. "Cursed be their anger, for it was fierce and their wrath, for it was cruel!" The anger you fail to control may lead you to a position whereby demonic forces are activated to inflict unnecessary sufferings against you in many areas of your life. You have a glorious destiny- Deal with Anger!

Aging

Aging is inevitable. However, we can slow down the process and retain more strength, vitality and beauty till later years if only we refuse to grow and nurture toxic emotions like anger. A wise man once said; it takes more muscles to frown than to smile. Anger makes one exert more force to the muscles which drain the energy in the body. People that get angry quickly look older than their actual age. Stay strong and beautiful- Deal with Anger!

WHAT TO DO WHEN YOU ARE ANGRY...

Admit it

"People who ignore their frustrated feelings often end up acting them out in a passive-aggressive manner."

Balestrieri

Without identification, there is no rectification. The first step to ensuring that anger does not control your life is to admit it. Tell yourself the truth. Allowing anger to simmer beneath the surface, refusing to admit it will lead to problems.

Seek God's face

"If we confess our sins, he is faithful and just and will forgive us our sins and purify us from all unrighteous."

1 John 1:9

After you have acknowledged that you are angry and figured out the source of it, the next step is to ask God to fix it for you. You can't do it on your own. Stay calm and stop trying to control everything. Remember Martha in Luke 10: 41-42, she was cumbered with many things that led to her frustration until she burst out "doest thou not care that my sister hath left me to serve alone." Just as the Lord Jesus had answered her, focusing on Jesus is the only antidote to anger, when it surfaces, God will settle it.

Let it slide...

"Forgiveness is the key to unlocking all the danger and hurt, the emptiness and darkness within. To unleash love, joy, fulfillment, and light inside."

-Zaneta Beverford

You need to forgive those who have in one way or the other hurt you. Let go of any angry feelings you are holding on to, and place those circumstances in God's hand.

"Be kind and compassionate to one and another, forgiving each other, just as in Christ God forgave"

Ephesians 4: 32

Think of the effect before expressing it.

"A gentle answer turns away wrath, but a harsh word stirs up anger."

Proverb 15:1

Be quick to listen and slow to speak. Responding to provocation with a harsh word only heightens the situation. However; a mild reply can often calm things down and defuse a tense situation.

Taking a little time off can help in limiting the anger you feel. When confronted with the trigger, make up your mind as soon as it occurs to pray about it, have a chat with a friend, engage yourself in domestic works or go for a short walk.

Bear the fruits of the spirit:

"But the fruit of the mind is love, joy, peace, patience, kindness. Goodness, faithfulness, gutlessness and self-control."

Galatians 5:22 -23

Did you at any point in this book feel you needed help with the way you express anger? Do you think your relationship would have been better if you could restrain yourself when provoked? Have you lost any opportunity or property due to a moment of rage? Don't you think you need some help right now?

Well, I want to inform you that Jesus can set you free from the seed and manifestation of uncontrollable anger. Accept him into your life today and receive the fruit of the Holy Spirit that accompanies this experience.

It is very difficult to be angry when you are an embodiment of love. It is hard to be upset when you are full of joy, when the peace of God reigns in you, when you have self-control and when you are as gentle as a dove.

Every seed needs to be watered to grow into a tree; however, the seed of anger needs to be killed immediately as the word of God does not permit it to remain until the sun sets.

"in your anger do not sin" do not let the sun goes down while you are still angry."

Ephesians 4:26

GOD BLESS YOU!

SPIRITUAL NUGGET 8

Anger is a gateway to so many problems. "It is one letter short of danger".

"Looking carefully lest anyone fall short of the grace of God; lest any root of bitterness springing up cause trouble, and by this many become defiled"

-HEBREW 12:15

CHAPTER NINE
THE SEED OF BITTERNESS

" Looking diligently lest any man fall of the grace of God; lest any root of bitterness springing up trouble you, and lest any man thereby many be defiled."

-Hebrews 12:15

The previous chapter was centered on diverse ways in which anger could penetrate our lives, an emphasis was made that anger is not necessarily evil, but its outcome could lead to sin. Also, there are various ways of dealing with anger, which involves admitting it, resolving it and letting it go. These were succinctly itemized and discussed.

Now! I will begin to explore another vital issue in this chapter that has eaten many lives away, caused more damage than healing, more pain than relieving, and more loneliness than friendship in our world today.

Without a doubt, life has never been fair. We come across lots of hurt virtually in our daily endeavors that keeps the heart panting for revenge. Imagine the job you spent years waiting to land in your hand, only to discover that it has been given to a new employee who you know not to be as qualified as you are. What about if your partner that you dearly loved, suddenly left you for someone else, after many years of struggles and suffering? The friend you trusted betrayed you by carting away the hard-earned savings that you had lent him or her in good faith. All these show that there are endless reasons why you deserve to spend the rest of your life in bitterness and resentment.

But wait a minute and have a second thought on this! The moment you're offended, you have a choice. You can choose to forget it and go on with the business of living, or you can choose to hold on to it. When you choose to hold on to it, a bitter root begins to grow and as it grows it begins to consume you like cancer, just as an American poet, singer and civil rights activist, Maya Angelou once said *"bitterness is like cancer. It eats upon the host."* Holding bitterness is walking in the flesh...sowing to the flesh and it will eat you up from the inside.

What is Bitterness?

"A bitter spirit will keep you from being a better person."

Woodrow Kroll

The word "Bitterness" comes from the Greek word, "Pikria," which means acridity, harshness, unhappiness, and irascibility. It results from an unsettled or unrequited frustration over anger or envy. It is an extended and intense hostility.

Bitterness is different from anger in the sense that anger is a spontaneous reaction to perceived intimidation or humiliation, while bitterness is a planned and purposeful reaction to the supposed action. Anger is about a present hurt; bitterness is about a past hurt. Bitterness lingers from something that happened in the past and overflows into all aspect of your life. Anger can be healed through forgiveness, but bitterness may be beyond your ability to absolve.

The soil of bitterness

In order for us to have in-depth knowledge of the root of bitterness, it is necessary to know the soil of bitterness that provides the environment which enhances the germination of the seed that gives rise to the root and fruit of bitterness.

The Bible represents soil with the heart. *"The seeds that fell along the path stand for those who hear, but the Devil comes and takes the message away from their* ***hearts*** *in order to keep them from believing and being saved."* (**Luke 8:12**)

The soil of bitterness is the heart that nurtured and nursed the incidents that happened to it with the hope of retaliating or withdrawing from such occurrence again. It is a heart that harbors hostility and does not deal with hurt by the grace of God. When someone becomes bitter, the bitterness takes root in the heart and grows deeper. It is the heart that wishes negative things to happen to the person that hurts them. The soil of bitterness brings discord. It allows or provides an environment for the root of bitterness to thrive.

The Root of Bitterness

"Lest any root of bitterness springing up trouble you, and lest any man thereby many be defiled."

-Hebrew 12:15b

Bitterness is a "root." It starts as a little tiny root hidden under the surface then suddenly grows to show its ugliness. It is easy to hide and conceal, therefore making it very difficult to detect. Just as the bitter water which the Israelites drank in Marah (Exodus. 15:23), its true nature is unknown until someone tastes of it. Hardly will you find anyone that will admit that they are bitter. They will either deny it or disguise it. Only after it has spread through that, the symptoms will then be seen as bitter words, thoughts, and deed.

It is glaring and hurting that bitterness is rampant in our families, society, and our churches today. Children are bitter towards parents. Parents are bitter toward children. The divorced are bitter toward their former spouses. Children of divorcees are bitter toward their parent's separation. Siblings are bitter over rivalries for parental affection and inheritances. Many loving families have been destroyed by the bitterness that came from the reading of a will.

There is bitterness in the workplace. Co-workers resent each other and their supervisors. There is class envy between employees and business owners. There is bitterness in the church. People are bitter toward their pastor. And, sadly, many pastors are bitter towards their church members. The worst of it all is that some are resentful toward God, His Word, and His Church. It has led them to commit some heinous acts. Bitterness between Christians over hurtful words, deeds, or attitudes is deadening and even causes disunity in churches.

The root of bitterness exists in two forms.

1) Bitterness towards people

2) Bitterness towards God

- Bitterness towards people

You may be embittered with people because of the wrong they have done to you; this can be people close to you. Just as I have earlier stated, bitterness is cloaked in nature. You may have it and not know. Perhaps these questions and reactions will help you out. How do you feel when someone who has offended you walks into the same room where you are in? Do you feel uncomfortable to the extent that you walk out of the room?

What about when you are opportune to meet someone that intentionally or unintentionally offended you, do you deliberately turn away to ignore and avoid him or her? When you hear about the success or progressive report of your EX, your employee or employer are you happy or resentful. Do you secretly desire calamity or failure–or worse–to come on that person? If your answer to this is yes! Then the root of bitterness is in you.

Let's see examples from the Bible

The Bible gives some illustrations of people who became cynical against their relatives and siblings just because of the favor they receive or what they possess.

The bitterness of Joseph's brothers was as a result of favoritism shown to Joseph by their father. Jacob openly loved Joseph more than any of his other sons, and he demonstrated it by giving Joseph a coat of many colors. Perhaps, a better description would be a robe that distinguished Joseph as being superior to his brethren.

"Now Israel loved Joseph more than all his children because he was the son of his old age and he made him a coat of many colors. And when his brethren saw that their father loved him more than all his brethren, they hated him, and could not speak peaceably unto him."

Genesis 37:3-4

It made his brothers envious and resentful towards him. And they were also envious of his dream. The Bible says " *when they saw him afar off, even before he came near unto them, they conspired against him to slay him and they said to one another, behold, this dreamer cometh*" (Genesis 37:18 -19).

Imagine how they termed their brother as 'This dreamer' Acts 7:9 says *"And the patriarchs, moved with envy, sold Joseph into Egypt"* The phrase 'moved with envy' refers to a burning emotion. It hurt them deeply, and it caused them to become angry and bitter.

As parents, you need to be cautious of how you display love to your children to avoid unnecessary competition that can sow the root of bitterness in them.

In second Samuel 13:1 -39, Absalom avenges the odious act his half-brother Amnon had done to his sister Tamar. He kept silent and feigned having forgiven Ammon for what he has done to Tamar; however unknown to Amnon, Absalom kept on nurturing, planning, plotting and scheming to murder him. After two years, he put him to death.

In Act 8:1 -23, Simon, the sorcerer was bitter because of the miracle wrought by Peter and John, he covets it and offered them money, but Peter perceived that his problem was bitterness.

"Repent therefore of this thy wickedness, and pray God, if perhaps the thought of thine heart may be forgiven thee, for I perceived that thou art in the gall of bitterness, and the bond of iniquity."

(Acts 8:23)

- Bitterness towards God

The first sign that reveals your bitterness towards God is when you often complain about your circumstances. If you allow bitterness to take hold of your heart, it will eventually come out of your mouth as murmuring and complaining.

Naomi felt resentful due to the death of her husband and sons. Eventually, she changed her name, Naomi, which meant *"Pleasant one"* to Mara, which is bitter one. This was because of the incident that occurred in her life.

Her life became bitter and filled with grief. She lost her spiritual edge, her troubles overwhelmed her and she held on to anger for all she had been through. Her bitterness reflected a heart of unbelief in the justice and sovereignty of God.

We read in Ruth 1:20-21 ***"And she said unto them, Call me not Naomi, call me Mara: for the Almighty hath dealt very bitterly with me. {21}, I went out full, and the LORD hath brought me home again empty: why then call ye me Naomi, seeing the LORD hath testified against me, and the Almighty hath afflicted me?"***

Perhaps you are also struggling with this same type of bitterness, thus making you question God and saying all manner of words to yourself. Indeed, it's common to blame God in times of grief and difficulty, but I want to let you know that God was in the midst of this situation even if she didn't see or feel it.

Have you allowed circumstances to make you bitter towards God? It is true that circumstances and situations will come that will be difficult for us to deal with, but the Bible says ***"Give thanks in all circumstances; for this is the will of God in Christ Jesus for you." (1 Thessalonians 5:18).***

You may be wondering why you are supposed to give thanks amid trials and temptations, but the Bible tells us to give thanks for the truth that God will use the circumstance for good. *"And we know that all things work together for good to them that love God, to them who are the called according to his purpose."*(**Romans 8:28**).

Nothing is a waste if given to God. We may not see the good come to fruition in our lifetime, it may be for an eternal good, but we can thank God for using it for His glory in some way. The trials and test are designed to make us better, not bitter.

EFFECTS OF BITTERNESS

Bitterness will affect you physically, emotionally, and spiritually because the fruit of bitterness is like an acid that destroys its container.

- Bitterness affects physically

"Bitterness does more harm to the vessel in which it is stored... then the vessel on which it is poured."

Anonymous

Researchers have shown that bitterness will undermine your physical health by engendering such problems as insomnia, high blood pressure, back pain, headaches, or abdominal condition. Also, it can raise your stress baseline, thereby taxing (or "overloading") your immune system.

Furthermore, Bitterness is medically linked to glandular problems, cardiac disorders, ulcers, and even insanity. It can lead to anxiety and depression, as well as insomnia. Our bodies don't like to be stressed all of the time, so these effects are ways in which our body let us know that it's not happy. The mind and the body affect each other.

Aside from the internal problems that bitterness can lead to, it can also lead to some external problems, like hostility and cynicism. It may seem very easy to be hostile or cynical.

- Bitterness affects emotionally

"Bitterness and resentment only hurt one person, and it's not the person we're resenting - it's us."

Alana Stewart

Bitterness brings sorrow, depression, and anger into a person's life. In the case of Esau, it drove him into a life of sin and immorality (Heb. 12:16).

Bitterness breaks down relationships and brings a sense of pessimism, futility, and unhappiness. Moreover, such a bleak, negative perspective prompts others to turn away from you. Loneliness is not far-fetched from bitterness. It prevents you from experiencing the potential joy of living fully in the present. Bitterness will cause your emotions to change at every point in time. You are easily influenced by the offenders. They dictate the tones of your emotion.

Furthermore, bitterness can also lead to trust issues and a loss of self-confidence. If you're bitter and cynical, then it's hard to trust others. You're always going to see something negative in them that will make you question their actions.

- Bitterness affects spiritually

"Bitterness never draws us closer to God."

Craig Groeschel

Bitterness is an open invitation to the devil. Through it, satan can enter into the life of a believer to control them. When your heart is bitter, you will find it difficult to see God for who He is because bitterness and holiness cannot dwell in the same heart. And without holiness, you will not see the Lord (Hebrews 12:14).

Bitterness can destroy your spiritual joy. It can destroy your witness with non-believers. It moves us away from God. It turns our heart away from God's grace and love.

"Looking diligently lest any man fails of the grace of God."

Hebrews 12:15

Bitterness can cause you not to experience the benefits of God's grace. It will devastate you spiritually because it necessitates that you walk in the flesh, and not in the spirit.

Bitterness is an open invitation to the devil. Through it, satan can enter into the life of a believer and control them. Also, bitterness grieves the Holy Spirit. It is in direct conflict with the fruit He desires to bear in our lives.

REMEDIES OF BITTERNESS

"Never succumb to the temptation of bitterness."

Martin Luther King, Jr.

Bitterness can keep you from moving forward and healing. And that can make it very hard for you to have fulfilling, healthy relationships, friendships, and experiences. And without those things, life is going to be difficult. So, how do you move beyond being bitter?

- Take it to God

"Come unto me, all ye that labor and are heavy laden, and I will give you rest."

-Matthew 11:28

Bitterness is like a burden that needs to be put off, if not, it will keep on accumulating until it weighs and breaks you down. Take it to God. He will lift the burden.

Admit that you feel bitter. Search deeply who hurt you and why you hold on to the hurt, and then take it to God in prayer.

- Forgive and Let it go.

"And be ye kind one to another, tenderhearted, forgiving one another, even as God for Christ's sake hath forgiven you."

-Ephesians 4:32

Forgive to be forgiven! Forgive, as Christ would forgive. Love like Christ would love. Walk like Christ. Talk like Christ. Although this is easy to suggest but hard to do, you've got to try and let go of resentment, anger, and whatever else preoccupies your thoughts.

"The medical evidence is clear and mounting. It's no exaggeration to say that bitterness is a dangerous drug in any dosage and that your very health is at risk if you stubbornly persist in being unforgiving."

Lee Strobel

Letting go of negative feelings can also help you forgive the person you be grudge. They may not deserve it, and you may not know how to do it, but that's okay. Take your time. Just working on forgiveness can lower stress and anxiety, strengthen your immune system, increase your self-esteem, lower blood pressure, and improve your other relationships.

"As we pour out our bitterness, God pours in his peace."

-F.B. Meyer

When you and I align our desires, motivations, wants, and beliefs with that of God, then we choose the better thing, not the bitter thing. Our godly desires lead to "betterness" as we get free of the whole "bitter mess."

Here are some examples of people who overcame bitterness in the Bible.

Joseph

Joseph had to let go of all the things he had experienced before he became the prime minister of Egypt. He had the cause to be bitter with how his brothers brutally dealt and sold him into slavery. His master's wife also placed false charges of rape on him. In all of these, he reconciled with his brothers because he saw the hand of God in his predicament.

"And Joseph said unto his brethren, I am Joseph; doth my father yet live? And his brethren could not answer him; for they were troubled at his presence.

And Joseph said unto his brethren, Come near to me, I pray you. And they came near. And he said, I am Joseph your brother, whom ye sold into Egypt. Now, therefore, be not grieved, nor angry with yourselves, that ye sold me hither: for God did send me before you to preserve life."

- Genesis 45:3-4

"But as for you, ye thought evil against me; but God meant it unto good, to bring to pass, as it is this day, to save many people alive."

-Genesis 50:20

The Bible says that all things work together for good to them that love God, to them who are the called according to his purpose. (Romans 8:28). It doesn't say that all things are good or that they are always enjoyable. It says that God can use all things to accomplish His perfect plan and purpose.

Hannah

Hannah was sorely provoked by Peninnah the second wife of her husband, Elkanah. Peninnah had children and purposely tried to make Hannah feel bad because she had no children. After years of Peninnah's unruly act, Hannah, became bitter to the extent that she refused to eat.

As time went by, she took her bitterness to the Lord in desperate prayer, openly confessing her grief, both to the Lord and to Eli, the priest. Finally, God heard her prayer and blessed her with a son- Samuel (1 Samuel 1: 1 - 28). By faith, Hannah gave her bitterness to the Lord, and because of it, she was able to return to her family, having been freed from sadness and was even able to eat normally. Later the blessings came: the Lord not only blessed her with Samuel, her firstborn who she gave to the Lord, but also with three other sons and two daughters.

Our Lord Jesus Christ

Think about how our Lord and Savior Jesus Christ endured all for our sake. Consider the bitter stripes across His back, the bitter nails that pierced His hands and feet; the bitter thorns driven in His head and the bitter words of people that wounded His loving heart. In spite of all this bitterness, hear Him say, *"...Father forgive them for they know not what they do"*(Luke 23:34)

Oftentimes, we deserve to be bitter because of the hurt that people have done to us, but we must always realize that forgiveness is the central Gospel of Jesus Christ. Without forgiveness, there would be no salvation. So if Jesus forgave us, shouldn't we forgive other people? So, do not carry or keep bitterness, but replace it with love, kindness, and forgiveness.

- ### Change your lens

Bitterness robs you of the hope and excitement for the future. If you find yourself drowning in self-hatred or self-blame, or thinking that you don't deserve happiness, let's make one thing clear: You deserve the absolute best in life. Without a doubt, you are not destined to be bitter. You can rise above this. Work on it. Be patient. Be kind to yourself and watch it work out.

Guide your heart

"Keep thy heart with all diligence; for out of it are the issues of life."

Proverbs 4:23

The heart is the recipient and processor of the events that happen to us. There is a need for you to monitor your heart and filter the information that can allow the root of bitterness to thrive in us. We need not only to be diligent concerning the condition of our heart; we equally consider the condition of our brothers and sisters in Christ lest they fall prey to the snare of bitterness.

"Never trust your tongue when your heart is bitter."

-Samuel J. Hurwitt

Whenever you choose a wrong desire based on a wrong belief, bitterness is likely to take root. God desires that we choose what He desires according to His plans and purposes.

Finally, bitterness is a sin that can destroy life, blow out the candle of joy, and leave the soul in darkness. It makes one unable to properly fellowship and serve the LORD.

It is true that circumstances and situations will come that will be difficult for us to deal with. They may cause us to become bitter if we do not handle them Biblically but recall that trials and testing are designed to make us better, not bitter.

We cannot forgive others until we have experienced the forgiveness of God. We do not deserve His forgiveness, but it is totally by grace that we are saved. "...Not of works...lest any man should boast..." Do you need the forgiveness of God today? If not, why not come and accept Jesus Christ as your Lord and Savior.

SPIRITUAL NUGGET 9

If you allow bitterness to take hold of your heart, it will eventually come out of your mouth as murmuring and complaining.

SEEDS OF DEFILEMENT

PART THREE
SEED OF WICKEDNESS

"In whom the god of this world hath blinded the minds of them which believe not, lest the light of the glorious gospel of Christ, who is the image of God, should shine unto them."

-2 CORINTHIANS 4: 4

"For rebellion is as the sin of witchcraft, and stubbornness is as iniquity and idolatry. Because you have rejected the word of the LORD, He has also rejected you from being king."

-1 SAMUEL 15:23

CHAPTER TEN
THE SEED OF WITCHCRAFT

"For rebellion is as the sin of witchcraft, and stubbornness is as iniquity and idolatry. Because thou hast rejected the word of the LORD, he hath also rejected thee from being king."

-1 Samuel 15:23

I'm glad you have made it to the last section of this life-transforming book. I know by now, you have had an incredible encounter with God in the previous chapters.

Now, this final section is centered on the seed of wickedness which includes the seeds of witchcraft, strife, and unforgiveness.

Interestingly, the Bible likens rebellion to witchcraft. This may sound surprising to you and you may wonder why a rebellious individual would be termed a witch or wizard. Well, I want you to open your mind to realize why God considers rebellion and Witchcraft as one and the same.

Evidently, we are living in a generation where the majority of those claiming to be Christians are walking, living, and acting in rebellion. Again, are you startled at this ugly reality? I'm not writing to make you feel bad.

However, from my experience as a Christian leader, counselor and pastor to thousands all over the world; I observe that rebellion, like witchcraft is not an attitude people would easily admit or repent from. Its seeds are subtle and its fruits are often hidden behind leaves of self-righteousness and vain glory.

So, won't you take some time to reflect and ascertain if this does not really apply to you? You might wonder why you need to be concerned about rebellion when you are a Christian. Well, you don't have to remind me of your devotion and service to God; I know you read your Bible and go to church, but, the question is, what do you do in between?

On the other hand, maybe you have not accepted Jesus as your personal Lord and Savior and yet, you have been reading this book from the beginning or the Lord has simply led you straight to this page after you 'strangely' picked up this life-changing book. This may get you thinking about the significance and implications of witchcraft and rebellion. I want to let you know that you are reading the book that will alter the course of your entire life for all the right reasons.

Keep reading...like your life really depends on it!

It is high time you pulled the blinders off. It's about time you make quality decision to measure up to what's in the Bible, instead of what is on your mind in this sinful world. It's about time you square up with God and ask Him to cleanse you from rebellion and witchcraft.

Rebellion, what is the big deal about it?

"For rebellion is as the sin of witchcraft."

-1 Samuel 15:23

The word rebellion in Hebrew is **"Marah,"** which means bitterness or provocation. That is to make or cause to be bitter. It is conscious disobedience to the express commands of God and human authority.

However, what is the similarity between rebellion and witchcraft. You see, the word "Witchcraft" in Hebrew is "qecem," meaning witchcraft or divination.

Certainly, at the root of rebellion is nothing more than willfully choosing to be led by a strange spirit. It means to do the will and work of the enemy in direct opposition to the will of God.

Furthermore, 1 Samuel 15:23 also stated that stubbornness is as iniquity and idolatry. Looking at this connection very well, you will realize that stubbornness is nothing but refusing correction and repentance; iniquity is nothing but sin and wickedness, and idolatry simply means choosing to give your service, obedience, and allegiance to a strange god?

You see, rebellion and divination will always lead people away from God, and without repentance, there is space for such a fellow in the camp of demons. This is why God rejected Saul as King over His people. He would not have a demoniac ruling over Israel-His chosen nation.

The seedlings of rebellion

"satan's tactics worked in heaven and they work on earth. He goes about spreading slander and rebellion."

-Derek Prince

Rebellion starts from the heart. It originates from a prideful heart. The first rebellion in the Bible was orchestrated by satan. He was made with precious stones but misplaced the golden opportunity by desiring to be like his creator.

"How art thou fallen from heaven, O Lucifer, son of the morning? How art thou cut down to the ground, which didst weaken the nations!

For thou hast said in thine heart, I will ascend into heaven; I will exalt my throne above the stars of God: I will also sit upon the mount of the congregation, in the sides of the north:

I will ascend above the heights of the clouds; I will be like the most High."

-Isaiah 14:12-14

Rebellion often goes along with envy. It makes its victims devise all means to ensure that someone in position of authority is removed, replaced, or calumniated. Its first point of manifestation is undue, unnecessary, and destructive criticism. It can also arise if people perceive that, they are being oppressed and that their right or interest is being subjugated.

Furthermore, rebellion often goes with fault finding, which then develops into nagging and murmuring against a system. People who lead rebellion are those who complain a lot, and at times they insist that things must be done according to their dictates.

Remember, there two significant forms of rebellion

- Rebellion against God
- Rebellion against the people in authority

Rebellion against God

"A creature revolting against a creator is revolting against the source of his own powers--including even his power to revolt. It is like the scent of a flower trying to destroy the flower."

-C.S. Lewis

Rebelling against God means knowing what God is expecting and requiring from you yet refusing to do it. In actual fact, it is choosing your way, comfort, satisfaction or pleasure ahead of God's will, principle and purpose for your life. It is common to find people who deliberately turn aside from God.

"Thus saith the LORD, Stand ye in the ways, and see, and ask for the old paths, where is the good way, and walk therein, and ye shall find rest for your souls. But they said we will not walk therein".

-Jeremiah 6:16

Rebellion against God's authority was humanity's first sin, which resulted in a fall and failure that lasted through many generations before Jesus came to redeem mankind. Adam and Eve were tempted by satan to eat from the fruits of a forbidden tree (tree of knowledge of good and evil).

The deceiver promised that, man would acquire a God-like wisdom and influence on the Earth with just one bite of rebellion. The devil refused to let them in on the loss, depravity, ignorance and pain that would follow.

"At the heart of all disorder, you will find a man in rebellion against God. It began in the Garden of Eden and continues to this day."

-Aiden Wilson Tozer

The nature of sin and satan is to take an opposing stance against any authority. The only way to live differently is to humbly embrace submission and reverence for spiritual and human authority. Submission is a protective covering from the scorching sun of human and divine judgment. God opposes the proud and rebellious. No nation takes treasonable offences lightly. God considers rebellion to be a form of demonic practice-witchcraft!

Rebelling against God means departing from God's instituted worship (Exodus 32: 8-9), neglect of His precepts (Daniel 9:5), refusal to listen (Deuteronomy 9:23), doubting his power (Ezekiel 17:15), and arrogant complain against Him (Number 20:3).

Conspiracy beneath the veil of discontent!

There was a time when the people of Israel journeyed in the wilderness to a promised land after a major deliverance from the hands of Pharaoh and the servitude in Egypt.

Israel and her leaders were greatly distressed by the conditions of the desert and the wanton cravings of the people. One day, thirst became a NATION-WIDE plague! Everyone wanted more water than they could find in the dry lands.

Instead of turning to God- Israel resorted to grievous complaining and murmuring that developed into much Chaos.

Then, God stepped in. Lovingly, He provided a solution. He instructed Moses to command the rock to yield water when the people of Israel complained of thirst (Number 20:1ff). He did as the Lord instructed but eventually went over and beyond divine instruction.

First, he rebuked the people, saying, "Listen, you rebels, second, he stood in place of God, "Shall WE bring water for you out of this rock?" Then, against God's directive to speak life to the rock; he indignantly struck that rock twice with his staff. Could this be the ROCK of Salvation?

God proved faithful and water gushed out in abundance from the rock (Num. 20:9-11), but that didn't resolve the act of disobedience of the people and now-Moses.

Don't be amazed! Partial obedience is total disobedience. You will later find out the implication of these gross deviation and disrespect in subsequent pages of this chapter.

Let's take a look at another scenario from the scriptures

There were times when Judges and Kings ruled Israel. Despite this, God was in-charge of leading her to battle for freedom and divine judgment against oppressive nations and wicked Kings that surrounded her.

One day, King Saul was directed by God to totally destroy the people of Amalekites and the wicked king Agag. God clearly stated:

"Now go and smite Amalek, and utterly destroy all that they have, and spare them not; but slay both man and woman, infant and suckling, ox and sheep, camel and ass."

(1 Samuel 15:3)

Instead of following God's directive Saul reserved the best of Amalekites' livestock and treasures to himself. Also, the wicked king Agag was preserved as a trophy of war. This was not in the original plan!

Even though, Saul disobeyed God's orders, yet Saul was pleased with his initiative and tried to justify his disobedience–the animals were to be sacrificed to the Lord, after all (verse 15). Aren't you like King Saul trying to cover your rebellion with flimsy excuses?

When a person rebels against God, everything God has created begins to work against such an individual. This clearly explains Prophet Jonah's experience with the violent Storm, wallowing Whale and Scorching sun.

In Jonah 1:1-7, God told Jonah to go and witness to the people of Nineveh. Jonah refused and boarded a ship to Tarshish.

On his way out of God's directives, everything began to work against him. First, it was the high wind on the sea; this wind almost broke the ship into two. Second, when the men on-board found that Jonah was the source of the problem, they bundled him and threw him into the sea. As if that was not enough, a big fish swallowed him and miraculously could not digest Jonah.

Rebellion against people in authority

The idea of being against authority has become the order of the day. In fact, some say that, if you do not question authority, then you are part of a corrupt system seeking to oppress people.

When there is rebellion against human authority, then, there is a rejection of the divine dominion ordained by God. Therefore rebelling against authority is tantamount to rebelling against God.

"And the LORD said unto Samuel, Hearken unto the voice of the people in all that they say unto thee: for they have not rejected thee, but they have rejected me, that I should not reign over them."

-1 Samuel 8:7

Miriam led a revolt against Moses (her brother and leader of the recently freed people of Israel), and she caught more than flu- she became leprous! Have you ever thought that leading rebellion to achieve personal ambition is the best way? Please, think differently!

You won't believe what happened to these guys: Korah, Dathan, and Abiram, who also rebelled against Moses' authority (Number 16: 1 -40). Moses prayed to God for vindication and in the end, the first ever EARTH QUAKE happened. 14,700 people were gulped into a wide opening under their feet! It was mysterious and many people learned their lesson!

Therefore, whenever you rebel against authority, you are equally rebelling against God.

John Chapter 3: 27, says a man can receive nothing unless it has been given to him from heaven. No one in the world today got into power without God's knowledge; this is why instead of complaining about a leader, you can report his errors to God.

God has laid the foundation

God is not an author of confusion; He has established chains of command. Every creature understands this.

"...the locusts have no king, yet all of them march in rank;"

-Proverbs 30:27

More so, Romans 13:1–7 instructs us to submit ourselves to the governing authorities, as long as those authorities do not require us to disobey the authority of God.

Rebellion against righteous authority leads to chaos and the dissolution of society. In the home, God's chain of power is that the husband is to be the shield, provider and head of the family. The husband's responsibility is to lead his family to the loving and gracious hands of Christ (Ephesians 5:23).

The wife is to submit to her husband, and children are to obey their parents (Ephesians 5:22; 6:1; Colossians 3:18, 20). Rebellion against familial authority also leads to chaos and dysfunction within the home.

Within the church, God has also created order. He has appointed elders to shepherd and keep watch over the congregation (1 Timothy 5:17; 1 Thessalonians 5:12; Hebrews 13:17). While elders or pastors are never to have absolute control over anyone, they are to be honored and obeyed as much as it is healthy for the church and the individual. Rebellion within a church leads to division and strife and a loss of effectiveness in carrying out God's mission (1 Corinthians 3:3).

By divine inspiration; Prophet Joel provided a good picture of a triumphant and Godly group. He said:

"They shall run like mighty men; they shall climb the wall like men of war; and they shall march everyone on his ways, and they shall not break their ranks:"

-Joel 2:7

Successful relationships and progressive associations must be rid of demonic influence spurred by witchcraft and rebellion.

DANGERS OF REBELLION

- Unfulfilled dreams

Moses and Aaron rebelled and were not allowed to enter into the Promised Land (Numbers 20:12-14, 27:14).

"Aaron shall be gathered unto his people: for he shall not enter into the land which I have given unto the children of Israel, because ye rebelled against my word at the water of Meribah,"

-Number 20:24

- Loss of position and possession

Saul was removed from being king, and the Holy Spirit withdrew from him (1 Sam 13-16). Also, Lucifer was cast out from his place in Heaven (Isa. 14:12-2; Ezekiel 28:11-19).

- Risk of life and property

Jonah was swallowed by a great fish (Jonah 1). He almost lost his life simply because of his disobedience, and this affected others to the extent of throwing their luggage to the sea.

- Loss of life

Immediately Judas Iscariot carried out his heinous acts, he went on to commit suicide. The priests were not spared from God's wrath on rebellion. Prophet Hananiah lost his life for his false prophesy.

"Therefore thus saith the LORD; Behold, I will cast thee from off the face of the earth: this year thou shalt die because thou hast taught rebellion against the LORD. So Hananiah the prophet died the same year in the seventh month"

-Jeremiah 28:16 -17

- It exposes someone to the works of the enemy

Those who commit rebellion will be delivered into the hands of the enemy. Since rebellion means turning away from the presence of God, God will allow the enemy to oppress and torment any person that wanders away from his or her place of rest.

"Nevertheless they were disobedient, and rebelled against thee, and cast thy law behind their backs, and slew thy prophets who testified against them to turn them to thee, and they wrought great provocations. Therefore thou delivered them into the hand of their enemies, who vexed them: and in the time of their trouble, when they cried unto thee, thou heardest them from heaven; and according to thy manifold mercies thou gavest them saviors, who saved them out of the hand of their enemies."

-Nehemiah 9: 26 -27

- Rebellion cuts a person off from God

Rebellion allows the god of this world, the devil to blind our spiritual eyes, and when our spiritual eyesight is blinded; our ability to discern is greatly affected.

"In whom the god of this world hath blinded the minds of them which believe not, lest the light of the glorious gospel of Christ, who is the image of God, should shine unto them."

-2 Corinthians 4: 4

REMEDIES FOR REBELLION

- Be humble enough to Seek God's face

"If my people, which are called by my name, shall humble themselves, and pray, and seek my face, and turn from their wicked ways; then will I hear from heaven, and will forgive their sin, and will heal their land."

-2 Chronicle 7:14

If you have been rebellious, it is high time you stopped! Forsake your rebellious acts and turn to the Lord so that you can receive the mercy of God. To get rid of rebellion, you need to submit every thought captive to the obedience of Christ. Sincerely, go to God, and humbly ask Him to forgive you of any kind of rebellion.

Subsequently, this means that when a negative thought comes, and you want to act it out in a certain way, you need to ask yourself, "Would Jesus act this way?

Henceforth, take every thought, every action, and every word to God in prayer. We need to regularly reflect to ensure that, our behaviors or actions line up with the Word of God.

Consistently ask, "Is this the Father's will for me?" You need to be persistent in prayer. Your life does not belong to you; it belongs to God, who should be seated on the throne of our choices and decisions. We should be in constant submission to Him.

- Focus on your innate ability

"And unto one, he gave five talents, to another two, and to another one; to every man according to his several abilities; and straightway took his journey."

-Matthew 25:15

Rebellion in church today has been rooted in one thing -Jealousy. God has graciously endowed very one of us with gifts to make remarkable progress in life. You are not to concern yourself with someone else's office, gift, or position. Don't envy others.

- Walk in humility

"Humble yourselves in the sight of the Lord, and he shall lift you up."

-James 4:10

Humble yourself under the shadow of the Almighty. Give honor to whom it is due. Rebelling against the people in authority is limiting your chances of getting to your position of leadership. We are advised to walk in meekness and in lowliness of mind. We are to walk in humility and also to recognize that all authority is God-given.

- Be thankful

"Oh that men would praise the LORD for his goodness, and for his wonderful works to the children of men."

-Psalms 107:8

An ungrateful heart is the beginning of rebellion. Francis Schaeffer once said *"the beginning of man's rebellion against God was and is, the lack of a thankful heart"*

Appreciate God for his goodness and mercy upon your life. Thank Him for what He has done, what He is doing and what He has in store for you. Never regret any day in your life but give glory to Him knowing that all things work together for good to everyone who loves God. (Romans 8:28)

May our heart never be turned away from the presence of God and may we remain steadfast in Him till He comes.

In Jesus Name!

Amen!

SPIRITUAL NUGGET 10

When there is rebellion against human authority, then there is a rejection of the divine dominion ordained by God. Therefore, rebelling against authority is tantamount to rebelling against God.

"For you are still carnal. For where there are envy, strife and divisions among you, are you not carnal and behaving like mere men?"

-1 CORINTHIANS 3:3

CHAPTER ELEVEN
THE SEED OF STRIFE

*"For ye are yet carnal: for whereas there is among you envying, and **strife**, and divisions, are ye not carnal and walk as men?"*

-1 Corinthians 3:3

A wise man once said, when two people think the same thing, the same way at the same time; without originality or reasonably different opinions; one of them is not thinking. Unity is not the same as holding one and a similar position in every situation. We must learn to have, hold, and express different ideas without negative feelings, rebellion, strife, or wickedness.

Can you take a moment to imagine how the world would be if relationships, marriages, workplaces, churches, and nations love freely, laugh heartily, relate closely, reach-out passionately, hug warmly, hold-hands sincerely and work diligently to resolve dividing issues and restore peace after every disagreement? This chapter will teach us how to achieve this!

Strife is cancer to the soul and strong hindrance to progress and unity among people. Take some time to examine relationships, families, communities, and gatherings where strife is eating deep into the fabric of harmonious co-existence; no one needs to look too deeply before they recognize the cracks on the walls and loud silence. It causes deafening ego, molds stiffed necks, leaves a sour taste, forms facial grimace, strong discontent, unnecessary strain, budding bitterness and irritable disagreement over certain or diverse issues in the hearts of everyone involved.

Oh! What a beautiful experience...

"Behold, HOW GOOD AND HOW PLEASANT it is for brethren to dwell together in unity!"

-Psalms 133:1

The text shows that it gladdens the heart of the Lord when we rejoice and do things in one accord. God's original intention for human relation **is** unity, peace, and harmony at every level.

We were created to live free from discord and conflict. When two people get together to talk without ill-feelings against one another, progress is inevitable, and God is pleased.

When a family worships God and prays with one heart in the beauty of holiness, there is no financial crisis, health issue, or any other daunting situation that can stand against them. With peace and unity, no mountain can be too high to move, nor Valley too deep to walk through or ocean too wide to swim across.

When people lift holy hands in one accord and call the God that answers prayer, He will respond at the speed of light and provide miracles that will testify to the fact that God is actively involved in their situation. (Matt. 18:20)

If the nation can come together, humble themselves and pray in spiritual harmony, setting aside their differences and conflict to reach out to the living God in one VOICE-They will be unstoppable! This is why, America and every other Nation on God's good Earth can find true freedom, restoration, healing and prosperity on a National scale when we all put strife away and touch heaven with one voice. Certainly, there is no telling what God can do for a UNITED NATION, FAMILY, CHURCH, BUSINESS, TEAM, or PEOPLE! (2 Chron. 7:18)

How did we get here?

Surely, there is no limit to what God can do when we get rid of seeds of strife and walk in unity. No other group of people experienced a clearer demonstration of God's power (despite ceaseless and severe persecutions) than the early Church. They were made of a strong and powerful unit of simple, ordinary, selfless, and likeminded people who loved God with all their heart.

The early Christians were spiritually in-sync and wholeheartedly connected. This was a major force with which they turned the world 'right-side-UP!' For Jesus Christ. Genuinely united and filled with the Holy Spirit, they didn't just survive, they thrived!

They preached the word of God with boldness, miracles, signs, and wonders followed their preaching. Thousands were being saved and added to the church, and many gave themselves, and their possessions for the Gospel of Jesus.

Hey! Come to think of it...why are we not frequently seeing the same power of God operating in our lives, family and the church today just as the early apostles and the church?

Remember, God is still the same! Hebrew 13: 8 says, "Jesus Christ the same yesterday, and today, and forever." Likewise, His hand is not weak to save; nor ear too distant to listen to our requests. Could discord and strife be an impediment?

First thing I want you to understand is the fact that God does not take sides! He is the rule and authority. He tells us what to do, and we are made to abide by His principles. Unity, harmony, and peace is God's way. When we step out of them into discord and strife, we set ourselves against God! How can anyone prevail against His Maker?

We have missed basic elements of divine involvement, such as love, fellowship, unity, and generosity; instead, we have put on the cloak of animosity, the garment of strife, helmets of hatred, voices that gossip and hearts that are divided. Certainly, where you find division, there is confusion and our God is not an author of confusion.

But, where did this wicked seed come from...

Remember that, fruits don't just show up...they start as seeds. Strife is a fruit or outcome of several errors. This book has been dedicated to helping you find heinous roots and vile seeds that produce defiling experiences, unpleasant outcomes, and negative fruits in your life.

The seed of STRIFE can be planted in the heart of any man or woman. When this seed germinates; he or she is left to suffer its painful and frustrating consequences.

Strife is a word coined out from Hebrew **"Madon"** and Greek **"Eris"** which means a contest, quarrel, uncertain affinity, contention, bitter disagreement, conflict. It usually arises from strong disagreements that lead to division, conflict, violence, vengeance, and every vile thing.

Strife is unnatural for people who are sensitive to God

"For where there is envy, STRIFE and DIVISIONS among you, are you not carnal and behaving like mere men?"

-1 Corinthians 3:3

If you have surrendered your life to Jesus Christ; you will become more sensitive to God through the help of the Holy Spirit, which now lives in you.

I want to let you in on the ONLY cause of strife in relationships based on Scriptures from the Bible. They are as follows:

PRIDE

"Only by PRIDE comes contention: but with the well advised there is wisdom."

-Proverbs 13:10

"He that is of a proud heart stirreth up strife..."

- Proverbs 28:25

The truth is numerous factors stirs up STRIFE! However, the seed of strife is primarily pride. Strife can be FUELED! It is like forest fire...It starts with a spark ego and flame of pride, which is eventually increased with more flammable attitudes or extinguished in the absence of provocative elements.

Before I talk about the place of pride and self-centeredness in the origin of strife; I want to share a few issues that keep the negative cycle of strife going in all kinds of relationships, be it, friendship, family, business, church, nation, or people.

First on the list is ANGER

"A wrathful man stirred up strife: but he that is low to anger appeased strife."

-Proverbs 15:18

Anger arises when a person perceives that his or her right has been tampered with or his or her expectation has not been met. Therefore, resentment and animosity begin to set in, resulting in strife with the offender. This was the reason the Bible warned that anger should not be allowed to see the setting of the sun before it is dealt with.

A perfect example is that which arose between Saul and David. When the Lord gave victory to the Israelites over the Philistines through David, there was celebration and jubilation in the whole city. The women came out to welcome King Saul with a song for the victory.

However, Saul's prideful heart shifted from the triumph to the accolade that was given to David. This made him angry, bitter and displeased, which eventually ended up in a conflict between them.

" And it came to pass as they came, when David was returned from the slaughter of the Philistine, that the women came out of all cities of Israel, singing, and dancing, to meet king Saul, with tabrets, with joy, and with instruments of music; And the women answered one another as they played,

and said, Saul hath slain his thousands, and David his ten thousand; And Saul was very wroth, and the saying displeased him; and he said, They have ascribed unto David ten thousand, and to me they have ascribed but thousands: and what can he have more but the kingdom? And Saul eyed David from that day and forward.

-1 Samuel 18: 6 – 9

Despite the fact that Saul was the anointed King of Israel, he had God's Spirit and favor upon on him yet; he became jealous of David's ability, success, and popularity among God's people. Instead of celebrating this huge success at this time, Saul allowed jealousy to grow in his heart. This led to disobedience and other sinful acts. The Bible says. "For wherever there are jealousy and selfish ambition, there you will find disorder and evil of every kind."

-James 3:16

Hatred

"Hatred stirreth up strife: but love covereth all sins."

-Proverb 10:12

When there is an intense dislike for someone, everything they do or say becomes inappreciable and disgusting. If this continues mutual coexistence and harmonious relationship will be stalled.

Provocative words

"A soft answer turneth away wrath: but grievous words stir up anger."

-Proverbs 15:1

Words can build or destroy relationships. This has been the cause for several separations and contentions in marriages, among business partners or just friends. Interestingly, some words that have been uttered can rarely be reversed.

Gossip

"Where no wood is, there the fire goeth out: so where there is no talebearer, the strife ceaseth."

-Proverb 26:20

Finally, I'm going to show you how literarily every STRIFE finds it's root in PRIDE, EGO, and SELF-CENTEREDNESS!

The Bible says:

"From whence come wars and fightings among you? Come they not hence, even of your lusts that war in your members? "

-James 4:1

Thinking too much about yourself will lead you speedily on a steep road to strife. Self-centeredness makes you solely consider how a situation affects you with little or no regard for areas where other individuals (s) are affected. A prideful person does not care about who feels hurt or what other people's perspective may be.

Selfishness and inordinate desire to outdo and outperform others is a major cause of unhealthy competition, bitter contention, and strife.

DANGERS OF STRIFE

1. Destroys unity

The Bible says "A house divided against itself cannot stand." Unity is one of the core successes of any endeavor. The achievement of two or more persons is stronger and better than an individual. Strive to be bonded and united in the love of God.

2. Strife hinders our progress and puts our lives on hold.

If there is no peaceful co-existence between people, how can they agree on things that will move them forward? If a husband and wife refuse to pull resources together, how would the family maintain lasting stability and have tremendous progress in the home? Amos 3:3 says; can walk together unless they agree. At times, strife can stand as a stumbling block to our breakthrough because of people we ought to meet for assistance, we may find it difficult to make our request known, due to the disagreement or discord we have with them. God will never answer a prayer that is offered with the contentious mind.

3. Loneliness

Nobody wants to stay around people that are contentious or live in a hostile environment. When people perceive that you are proud, a gossip or too adamant, they will cut any relationship they have with you.

4. Broken home

"It is better to dwell in the corner of the housetop, than with a brawling woman in a wide house."

-Proverbs 21:19

Whenever there is a disagreement between husband and wife, and if this is not settled amicably, it may cause the family to split apart. Eventually, the family decisions will no longer be made together between the couple.

5. Hinders an individual from getting into heaven.

"Envying, murders, drunkenness, revellings, and such like: of which I tell you before, as I have also told you in time past, that they which do such things shall not inherit the kingdom of God."

-Galatians 5:21

In all our tasks and endeavors on earth, Heaven should be our goal and focus. Endeavor to live according to the standard of the creator so that you can inherit the kingdom of God. Strive to live a life that is pleasing by ruling out every work of the flesh as listed in the Galatians 5:21.

HOW TO DEAL WITH STRIFE

Strife is designed to destroy our lives, our relationships, and even the church of God. We must not fail to stand up to it. When it rises against us, we must actively resist it by following these principles.

1. Deal with it as it comes

You don't have to yield to envy and strife! When the opportunity for strife arises, choose to always make room for the ideas, thoughts, and opinions of others. Abraham knew how deadly strife is and diffused the situation with the wisdom of God. Let's take a look at this scenario.

When Abraham left the Land of Ur of the Chaldeans to the land of Canaan as God commanded him. He left with his wife (Sarah) and his Nephew (Lot) to the land of Canaan (Genesis 12:5). Abram was very rich in cattle, silver, and gold. Likewise, Lot had flocks and herds (Genesis 13:1ff)

However, it got to a point where Abraham and Lot's herds grew so large that the land which they dwelt in could not contain them.

"...The land was not able to bear them, that they might dwell together: for their substance was great, so that they could not dwell together. And there was a strife between the herdsmen of Abram's cattle and the herd men of Lot's cattle: and the Canaanite and the Perizzite dwelled then in the land.

-Genesis 13: 6-7

As a result, strife arose between the herdsmen of Abraham and that of Lot over the best grazing land for their livestock. Abraham saw this strife and said, *"Let there be no strife between you and me, and between your herdsmen and my herdsmen, for we are kinsmen" (Gen 13:8).*He graciously gave Lot the choice of which land to use for his livestock, thereby diffusing the conflict between their herdsmen in a magnanimous way.

This single act of Abraham prevented an escalation of the issue which the Canaanites and Perizzites might have capitalized on to destroy both families since disunity exposes a weakness.

By maintaining an attitude of staying on the same side with your fellow believers, you can put the devil on the run and keep your relationships alive, healthy, and long-lasting!

2. **Be kind and gentle.**

"Pleasant words are a honeycomb, sweet to the soul and healing to the bones."

-Proverbs 16:24

It is worthwhile to give kudos to Abraham for his diplomatic approach in handling the issue. His words to Lot were neither harsh nor confrontational. They were gentle and kind. He emphasized that they were family, and strife should not exist between family members. Thus, he offered a solution which minimized the chance of the conflict from escalating. Christians are expected to demonstrate gentleness and patience when dealing with other people (2 Timothy 2:24; Titus 3:2; Romans 12:18).

3. **Thinking of others as better than you.**

"Let nothing be done through strife or vainglory, but in lowliness of mind let each esteem other better than themselves."

-Philippians 2:3

The place of humility cannot be overemphasized. It drives away Selfishness and self-centeredness. From our story, we could see that Abram humbled himself and showed great mercy, love, patience, and grace to Lot. He was the elder and had the right to demand what part of the land he would take. Abram, even more importantly, was the one to whom God had promised the land, not Lot. Rather than making the demands and claiming the part he wanted, Abram showed great humility and allowed Lot to choose. He saw his relationship with Lot and his reputation with the rest of the world to be a much more precious thing to pursue than the best part of the land and his rightful standing in the family.

Abram's humility and wisdom in this situation are attributes we should all desire. They are not natural to us and are typically fruits that grow from many years of mistakes and pain to reach this level of maturity. This should be a daily prayer that God would grow us to be more humble, wise, meek, and peace-seeking with those whom we disagree or feel wronged by.

4. **Be a peacemaker**

"Follow peace with all men, and holiness, without which no man shall see the Lord."

-Proverbs 12:14

Don't confront people with the aim of fighting or quarreling. Always find a solution to any situation you find yourself in rather than intensifying it.

Abraham's solution to bring peace involved allowing Lot to first choose where to settle. Lot jumped at this opportunity to take the best land for himself. Abraham had to take the less fertile land because of his offer to maintain peace. One of the aspects of godly wisdom is being "willing to yield" (James 3:17). Sometimes it is necessary for us to take a personal loss–in other words, make a sacrifice–for the sake of peace with others.

We should seek peace and unity with others as far as it does not lead us to sin or compromise. We should make peaceful resolutions and set aside our desires for one another but never at the expense of the Gospel.

5. Be content

Appreciate God for what he has done for you and rejoice with other people that are celebrating rather than grumbling. Put your hope in God and His will. Believe He can do more than what you have asked from him.

6. Be comfortable with other people's progress

Saul was embittered because of David's fame and success, and this led to his downfall. He allowed the devil to control and direct his action. It is true that we may not have gotten what we needed at a particular time, but we should cast all our burdens on Him for He cares for us. Never regret any situation you find yourself. Also, don't be envious of other people's success; there is so much space in the sky for everyone to fly.

7. Pray

Prayer is a powerful force that can settle a matter. It is what connects divinity with humanity. It is like a lifeline. Therefore, use this means to combat strife. Earnestly pray for the power of God and the fruit of the spirit so that you can remain steadfast in Christ Jesus.

SPIRITUAL NUGGET 11

With peace and unity, no mountain can be too high to move, no valley too deep to walk through or ocean too wide to swim across.

"If you want people to like you, forgive them when they wrong you. Remembering wrongs can break up a friendship."

-PROVERBS 17:9

CHAPTER TWELVE
SEED OF UNFORGIVENESS

"If you want people to like you, forgive them when they wrong you. Remembering wrongs can break up a friendship."

-Proverbs 17:9

Glory to God! This is the last Chapter of this book. It will help you understand unforgiveness and its seed. You will be provided with Biblical principles and life practices that will help you find it easy to forgive even the most grievous offense that has been intentionally or carelessly directed against you.

You see, all forms of healthy relationships, friendships, and fellowships are beautiful gifts from God. He looked carefully at Adam one day and said it wasn't a good thing for him to be alone. So, God created Eve, who became Adam's companion. We were made for and not against one another.

Can you for a moment just try to imagine how boring life would be if you were to live alone in your city having all the good stuff like houses, cars, food, and all the designer clothes but no real people around to share and enjoy life with? Life can be empty without love and friendship.

It is usually a magnificent sight when people from a different family background connect so intimately with one another and become best of friends. Laughter, fun, and generous gifts are effortlessly shared in an atmosphere of love and unbroken fellowship.

Then "Boom!" Something terrible happens between people who could have been friends for life! Someone gets deeply hurt, and best friends become sworn enemies who can no more bear to stand the sight of each other. What seed would produce such thorns of hate, defiled conscience, and grow thistles of discord among people? Can there be any kind of relationship without occasions for offense? Can we really have good friends, colleagues, relatives, partners, couples, and neighbors for life?

You see, marriages thrive on love and forgiveness. It is not uncommon to find scenarios when marital relationships suddenly turn sour. It is not a strange sight to see two seemingly love-birds take-ups on each other and drag partners before a court of law to secure divorce or separation. In most cases, this is because one or both parties has decided not to forgive the offender for a perceived wrong or injustice.

Similarly, some nations of the world consider other nations as their enemies. In most cases, it is usually due to an event that once transpired in history, even when the generation of people who witnessed the event had been long gone. For example, Israel and Palestine are enemies, and it doesn't seem any type of diplomacy can ever erase that.

I'm sure you won't be surprised to realize that believers who are the members of the body of Christ are not exempted from holding grievances against one another. Certainly, the church comprises a group of people who love God but are also prone to mistakes and vulnerable to imperfections.

However, this is God's word to the church as spoken by Apostle Paul:

"And be ye kind one to another, tenderhearted, forgiving one another, even as God for Christ's sake hath forgiven you."

-Ephesians4:32

In the above scripture, Paul the apostle is urging the brethren in the Ephesian church and by extension, every member of the body of Christ (which includes you and me) to forgive one another.

What is forgiveness?

Forgiveness can be defined as a conscious and deliberate decision to release feelings of resentment or vengeance toward a person or group who has harmed you, regardless of whether they actually deserve it or not.

Unforgiveness is a decision to hold on to hurts and pain from an event that transpired with an individual or group of people and to resist any means of reconciliation.

Unforgiveness, like any other carnal tendency, starts as a seed, takes root, extends branches, and develops the unpleasant fruits and negative experiences in the life of anyone who permits it.

WHERE DOES UNFORGIVENESS COME FROM?

First, what's your take on a lack of remorse...?

"But he would not listen to her, and since he was stronger than she was,

HE OVERPOWERED HER AND RAPED HER.

Then Ammon was filled with a deep hatred for [Tamar]; he hated her now even more than he had loved her before. He said to her, "Get out!"

"No," she answered. "To send me away like this is a greater crime than what you just did!" But Ammon would not listen to her; he called in his personal servant and said, "Get this woman out of my sight!

THROW HER OUT AND LOCK THE DOOR!"

-2 Samuel 13:14-17

"I am sorry!" is a three worded sentence that has proven to be very powerful in softening the hardest heart and extinguishing the fiercest of wrath and rage. However, in most cases, people need a lot of genuine courage and true humility to come to a point when releasing themselves from obstinate stance even when they are wrong. How easily do you to admit a wrong and offer remorseful apologies?

Imagine after being clearly hurt by an individual, and the person still ends up displaying arrogant and nonchalant attitude over the issue? You can relate to the sense of injustice, anger, and frustration that comes with a lack of remorse. The truth is, some people often make offering forgiveness a bit challenging.

So, what happens when you have not been able to overcome the pain from the hurt you suffered and now you still have to bear arrogance and over bloated ego from the people who should be down on their faces asking for your forgiveness? What can you do to live free form hate and bitterness against everyone every time?

Understandably, some people cannot stand a lack of remorse, and this is where they "throw in the towel," languish in hate, conceive ill-feelings and sever valuable relationships.

Dealing with hurtful memories that don't just go away...

"When David was about to die, he called ... Solomon and gave him his LAST INSTRUCTIONS: [he said]... you REMEMBER what Joab did to me by killing the two commanders of Israel's armies, Abner, son of Ner and Amasa son of Jether. You REMEMBER how he murdered them in time of peace as revenge for deaths they had caused in time of war. He killed innocent men, and now I bear the responsibility for what he did, and I suffer the consequences.

You know what to do; you must not let him die a natural death...

"There is also Shimei... [Who] cursed me bitterly the day I went to Mahanaim, but when he met me at the Jordan River, I gave him my solemn promise in the name of the LORD that I would not have him killed.

But you must not let him go unpunished. You know what to do, and

YOU MUST SEE TO IT THAT HE IS PUT TO DEATH."

-1Kings 2:1, 4-9

Our memory can be a powerful treasure or a dangerous dungeon. Keeping records, journals, and memorials of past hurts, offenses, and offenders can be helpful and hurtful at the same time. Despite that, record keeping is a beneficial and important habit; however, not all events deserve to be kept in the archive of our mind. Maintaining a record of dates and events when you were offended can be very unsafe and capable of breeding bitterness and festering hatred!

A lot of people are in the habit of keeping diaries and journals of the hurt done against them, they also take, replay and retain pictures that bring sad memories and messages.

Sincerely, some memories never go away! Yet, we can choose to deal with hurtful recalls by renewing our mind with the word of God and prayer. There are other practical ways of dealing with offenses which will be discussed later in this Chapter Please, keep reading!

Justice delayed can become Justice denied...

Genesis 34:1-2 One day Dinah, the daughter of Jacob and Leah, went to visit some of the Canaanite women.

When Shechem the son of Hamor the Hivite, who was chief of that region, saw her, he took her and raped her.

Genesis 34:5 Jacob learned that his daughter had been disgraced, but because his sons were out in the fields with his livestock, HE DID NOTHING UNTIL THEY CAME BACK.

Genesis 34:7 just as Jacob's sons were coming in from the fields. When they heard about it, they were shocked and furious that Shechem had done such a thing and had insulted the people of Israel by raping Jacob's daughter.

Gen 34:25-31 Three days later, when the men were still sore from their circumcision, two of Jacob's sons, Simeon and Levi, the brothers of Dinah, took their swords, went into the city without arousing suspicion, and killed all the men, including Hamor and his son Shechem. Then they took Dinah from Shechem's house and left.

After the slaughter, Jacob's other sons looted the town to take revenge for their sister's disgrace.

They took the flocks, the cattle, the donkeys, and everything else in the city and in the fields.

They took everything of value, captured all the women and children, and carried off everything in their houses.

Jacob said to Simeon and Levi, "YOU HAVE GOTTEN ME INTO TROUBLE; now the Canaanites, the Perizzites, and everybody else in the land will hate me. I do not have many men; if they all band together against me and attack me, our whole family will be destroyed."

BUT THEY ANSWERED,

"WE CANNOT LET OUR SISTER BE TREATED LIKE A COMMON WHORE."

The desire to see justice done resides in every normal human being. This is because we were created in the image of a God who is righteous and just. This is why it is usually heartbreaking to see a wicked person walking about freely without retribution.

Take some time to read that interesting story under this subheading, and you will find that, the children of Jacob could not live with the thought that their father would not avenge the rape of Dinah, their sister. So, they maliciously took vengeance on their own without any regard for the consequences.

DANGERS OF UNFORGIVENESS

Prepare for surprises

I'm sure you now realize that unforgiveness can breed disaster, like a time bomb waiting to go off! There is a thin line between unforgiveness and bitterness. As soon as the threshold is crossed or a trigger has been pulled, or a situation has given way for vengeance, malice, damage, and destruction; you can hardly predict what would happen next!

Absalom eventually killed Ammon, and some of his brothers who he perceived could be a threat. Simeon and Levi disseminated a whole city because they wouldn't let their sister's rape lie in the grave of past memories. David meticulously left a hit-list against all his past enemies.

You can also relate and recall one or two occasions where you lashed out violently or reacted in an unfriendly manner to people who have previously hurt you. One thing you will recognize and remember is the fact that most of your negative reactions and actions were somewhat unexpected (especially in magnitude) and you probably felt embarrassed by your actions, leaving you with a thought that goes like-"Where did this come from?" The seed of unforgiveness can yield disastrous fruits. BEWARE! You might end up doing something you will later regret.

At the least, unforgiveness will damage relationships

Once again, remember that relationship is everything. No one can truly exist without direct and indirect forms of contact, coherence, collaboration, and communication with other people. However, when offenses creep into any kind of relationship, they become sour and toxic. Unforgiveness often turn out to be defilers and poisons, which works death and destruction in every direction.

satan's goal is to keep people separated and disharmonious. This way, he can creep in and destroy individuals who could have been protected if they were under the covering of Godly relationships.

The enemy understands the enormous power and multiplier effect of harmony, synergy, and unbroken fellowship. satan can neither stand the light of love nor resist the force of unity.

I will talk more about the power of good and Godly relationships and why you must guard them with all you've got.

Finally, unforgiveness will strain your health in every ramification

Beloved, you deserve a sound physical, balanced emotional, mental, and spiritual health. You don't need to drain or strain your wellbeing by harboring unforgiveness. All you need to do is identify areas where holding on to an offense could be placing demands on your mental concentration, emotional stability, physical health, and spirituality.

Unforgiveness results in anxiety and tension at every thought and remembrance of the hurtful event. Have you ever looked at a person who once offended you and felt so uneasy around him or her?

In a recent study, it was discovered by Dr. Michael Barry that 61% of the cancer patients he examined had forgiveness issues. This is because chronic anxiety in all respects typically produces overabundant adrenaline and cortisol, which drain the creation of natural killer cells, which is your body's defense in the battle against malignant growth of cancer.

It can lead to despair and depression: The individual you have sworn never to forgive many times isn't aware of your resolve, but the weight of unforgiveness you carry will pull your soul down. You won't be able to think straight and properly any time you recall the event or see the person responsible.

HOW TO OVERCOME UNFORGIVENESS

Accept forgiveness

"The servant fell on his knees before the king. 'Be patient with me,' he begged, and

I WILL PAY YOU EVERYTHING!"

-Mathew 18:26

You cannot give what you don't have. God is the ultimate source of forgiveness, and as long as you refuse to surrender your life to Jesus and accept His forgiveness for your endless and grievous sins, you will not be able to release forgiveness to people.

Several people love to relate to God based on works, reward, and punishment. The danger here is, we often relate to people based on our salient or pronounced perception of who God is to us. When you believe that you have been forgiven unconditionally, the only thing you want to do is forgive people with the same love and kindness that has been extended to you.

However, if you go around with the same mindset as people who try to pay for their sins, then you will likely want to have other people pay for what they have done against you.

Jesus told a parable about the Kingdom of God which revealed that the Father wants to relieve us from all consequences and absolve all our trespasses without any reservation. Sadly, many people are currently responding like the servant who said: "Boss! Give me some more time; I WILL PAY YOU EVERYTHING I OWE". The unfortunate reality is, you cannot pay back enough for your sins and offenses against God. Why then would you expect people to pay back for their offenses against you fully?

You must take time to reflect over the love of God and how greatly you have been forgiven so you can learn to show mercy and forgiveness to people regardless of their offenses against you.

Value relationships

"So if you are about to offer your gift to God at the altar and there

YOU REMEMBER THAT YOUR BROTHER HAS SOMETHING AGAINST YOU, leave your gift there in front of the altar, go at once and make peace with your brother, and then come back and offer your gift to God."

-Matthew 5:23-24

Unforgiveness can influence us in diverse ways. However, the fundamental evidence of keeping a grudge or taking an offense against someone is a break in a cordial relationship. Most of the time, we don't seem to worry too much about someone somewhere who may to be crossed with us. Maybe because we assume we don't need that relationship after all!

Please note that forgiveness is not appropriate for greasing wrong relationships. It is meant for valuable fellowship and permissible associations. Jesus always connects forgiveness with a BROTHER [or SISTER]. This is no one else but someone with whom we share good and Godly ties and spiritual covenant through the blood of Jesus.

Trust me when I say, study the Word as to be wise in regard to choosing the right people to keep company with. That way the people you are close to wouldn't offend you in the first place. An unbeliever should not be intimate friends with certain people as to the point that you begin to allow their actions to affect you so significantly. Guard your heart.

Until someone is born again, he or she will remain in darkness and under the influence of the enemy-satan, what would you expect from someone in this pitiable condition? Should you become angry despite the fact that you know they don't entirely comprehend or deeply understand the root or implications of their actions against you?

You see, if they knew better- they would do BETTER! Like Jesus and Stephen, who prayed for sinners that persecuted and abused them. Don't ever forget to say: "Father, forgive them [that resentful colleague at work, abusive spouse, dubious business person, unfair superior and more] FOR THEY KNOW NOT WHAT THEY ARE DOING!"

The truth is there are toxic, unhealthy, ungodly, vain, and hurtful relationships. You can get hurt and offended when you relate with the wrong crowd. The good thing is when you can identify the error in such unwholesome association or relationships, turn your pain to purpose, redirect your focus, and rediscover true friendship.

If you tolerate hurtful and toxic relationships and you call that forgiveness; soon you might be rudely awakened to the fact that you have probably ruined a significant portion of your life through lack of discernment or vain pleasure.

Nonetheless, I want to challenge you to treasure and take care of wholesome relationships that God has placed in your life. Whenever misunderstandings or offenses creep in, do not hastily destroy the bridge, block them out, and turn your back; you might be missing something special. God has strategically placed people in our lives; some as Christian friends, colleagues, marriage partners, leaders and many more, who were destined to take us from where we are to our next level in business, career, family, love and walk with God.

You won't believe it if I tell you that often times, God in His glory and grace encourages us to give preference to our relationships with people (regardless of their fault or failures) above offering hypocritical gifts or remaining hurt, miserable and frustrated in His presence. Usually, the condition of our relationship with people will influence the state of our heart towards God and the blessing attached to the unbroken fellowship with Him.

Prioritize Communication

"If your BROTHER sins against you go to him and SHOW HIM HIS FAULT..."

-Matthew 18:15

"And Absalom hated Amnon so much for having raped his sister Tamar that he would no longer even SPEAK TO HIM."

-2 Samuel 13:22

This is another key that unlocks forgiveness, an action that removes bitterness and attitude that releases Grace when offenses try to strain relationships. That is COMMUNICATION. While it true that, our first reaction to hurts and offenses is to block out the offender and avoid any form of contact or communication; however, there is no way out of unforgiveness without effective and sincere communication. Don't assume or suggest more reasons why the offender should be intuitively aware of what they did that hurt you, instead follow the Jesus-way which is to SPEAK OUT!

In Mathew Chapter 18, verses 15; Jesus is saying: "Never remain hurt and silent." Find a way to "SHOW HIM/HER HIS/HER FAULT."

This implies that sometimes people don't know when, where, or how much they have offended you. It is easy to wait until the offender realizes what he or she has done, but if you must be free from unforgiveness, you need to swim against the tides.

To know more about how to resolve issues with people by leveraging on the power of communication and active involvement; read Matthew 18: ....

Have a large heart

"Then Peter came to Jesus and asked, "Lord, if my brother keeps on sinning against me, how many times do I have to forgive him? Seven times?"

-Matthew 18:21

It is important that we recognize the limitation of humans in our dealings every day. Even a well-meaning person can still end up disappointing you when he never intended to.

Certainly, offenses will come, but the responsibility is on you to let it slide as it comes. Having a large heart will make us let go of something we thought we would never forgive. We should forgive unconditionally and unilaterally whether the person comes to ask for forgiveness or not.

Read and meditate on God's word:

"Wherewithal shall a young man cleanse his way?

By taking heed thereto according to thy word."

-Psalms 119:9

There is no better way to purify the human heart from all forms of influences than the Word of God. The Word of God is quick, powerful, and sharper than any double-edged sword. It can perform delicate heart surgery and remove all impurities of the spirit, soul, and body.

Pray to God for the healing:

"Is any among you afflicted? Let him pray. Is any merry? Let him sing psalms."

-James 5:13

Unforgiveness is a heavy burden to carry. The pains in your heart, the thoughts of shame that won't leave your head, the bitterness, resentment, and anger that you feel can be taken away by God if you ask him through prayer.

"For if ye forgive men their trespasses, your heavenly Father will also forgive you: But if ye forgive not men their trespasses, neither will your Father forgive your trespasses."

-Matthew 6:14

God Bless You!

Be free! Stay Free!

SPIRITUAL NUGGET 12

When you believe that you have been forgiven unconditionally, the only thing you want to do is forgive people with the same love and kindness that have been extended to you.

CONCLUSION

Seeds are not only sown in earthly soil but also in the human heart. These seeds are in the form of what we hear and see which become words and images.

Whatever we listen to and see is absorbed in our hearts and begins to reproduce and form us. It is your responsibility to carefully choose what you see and pay attention to; because this is one way in which the devil tries to get an inroad into our lives.

Therefore, guard your heart diligently because out of it flow the issues of life.

I believe that this book has been a blessing to you. My prayer is that you will continually live a life of victory above the target of the devil.

The goal of Messengers of Fire Ministries is to impact lives and lead many souls into the kingdom of God. My wife and I have made a commitment to lead souls into all truth - just as Jesus Christ has taught us.

Saints, these truths that you have read are faithful. Let love be the foundation for our ministry into your hearts and mind for the rest of your life.

Janet and I would like to thank you all from the bottom of our hearts for reading this book...Messengers of Fire Ministries loves you all.

SCRIPTURE OUTLINE

INTRODUCTION

"And God said, let the earth bring forth grass, the herb yielding seed, and the fruit tree yielding fruit after his kind, whose seed is in itself, upon the earth: and it was so."(Genesis 1:11)

"Thou shalt not sow thy vineyard with divers seeds: lest the fruit of thy seed which thou hast sown, and the fruit of thy vineyard, be defiled." (Deuteronomy 22:9)

"But while men slept, his enemy came and sowed tares among the wheat, and went his way."(Matthew 13:25)

"That which is born of the flesh is flesh; and that which is born of the Spirit is spirit"(John 3:6)

"Now the works of the flesh are manifest, which are these; Adultery, fornication, uncleanness, lasciviousness, Idolatry, witchcraft, hatred, variance, emulations, wrath, strife, seditions, heresies, Envying, murders, drunkenness, revellings, and such like: of the which I tell you before, as I have also told you in time past, that they which do such things shall not inherit the kingdom of God."(Galatians 5:19-22)

CHAPTER 1

"All things were made by him [God]; and without him was not anything made that was made."(John 1:3)

"And the serpent [satan] said unto the woman, ye shall not surely die: For God doth know that in the day ye eat thereof, then your eyes shall be opened, and ye shall be as gods, knowing good and evil." (Genesis 3:4-5)

"Thou art worthy, O Lord, to receive glory and honor and power: for thou hast created all things, and for thy pleasure they are and were created."

(Revelation 4:11)

"Their land also is full of idols; they worship the work of their own hands, that which their own fingers have made." (Isaiah 2:8)

"Their end is destruction; their god is their stomach; their glory is in their shame. They are focused on earthly thing." (Philippians 3:19)

"But every man is tempted, when he is drawn away of his own LUST, and enticed. Then when lust hath conceived, it bringeth forth sin: and sin, when it is finished, bringeth forth death." (James 1:14-15)

"And when he sowed, some seeds fell by the way side, and the fowls came and devoured them up." (Matthew 13:4)

"But seek ye first the kingdom of God, and his righteousness; and all these things shall be added unto you." (Matthew 6:33)

"Keep thy heart with all diligence; for out of it are the issues of life." (Proverbs 4:23)

"Finally, brethren, whatsoever things are true, whatsoever things are honest, whatsoever things are just, whatsoever things are pure, whatsoever things are lovely, whatsoever things are of good report; if there be any virtue, and if there be any praise, think on these things." (Philippians 4:8)

"This know also, that in the last days perilous times shall come. For men shall be lovers of their own selves, covetous, boasters, proud, blasphemers, disobedient to parents, unthankful, unholy, Without natural affection, trucebreakers, false accusers, incontinent, fierce, despisers of those that are good, Traitors, heady, high minded, lovers of pleasures more than lovers of God;" (2 Timothy 3:1-4)

"Put to death therefore what is earthly in you; sexual immorality, impurity, passion, evil desire, and covetousness, which is idolatry." (Colossians 3:5)

"Let your conversation be without covetousness; and be content with such things as ye have: for he hath said, I will never leave thee, nor forsake thee." (Hebrews 13: 5)

"And he said unto them, Take heed, and beware of covetousness: for a man's life consist not in the abundance of the things which he possess." (Luke 12:15)

"And Achan answered Joshua, and said, indeed I have sinned against the LORD God of Israel, and thus and thus have I done: When I saw among the spoils a goodly Babylonish garment, and two hundred shekels of silver, and a wedge of gold of fifty shekels weight, then I coveted them, and took them; and, behold, they are hid in the earth in the midst of my tent, and the silver under it." (Joshua 7:20-21)

"This he said, not that he cared for the poor; but because he was a thief, and had the bag, and bare what was put therein." (John 12:6)

"Marriage is honorable among all, and the bed undefiled; but fornicators and adulterers God will judge ..." (Hebrews 13:4)

CHAPTER 2

"Marriage is honorable in all, and the bed undefiled..." (Hebrews 13:4)

"Keep thy heart with all diligence; for out of it are the issues of life. (Proverbs 4:2)

"Some time passed. David's son Absalom had a beautiful sister named Tamar, and David's son Amnon was infatuated with her. Amnon was frustrated to the point of making himself sick over his sister Tamar because she was a virgin, but it seemed impossible to do anything to her. Amnon had a friend named Jonadab, a son of David's brother Shimeah. Jonadab was a very shrewd man, and he asked Amnon, "Why are you, the king's son, so miserable every morning? Won't you tell me? " Amnon replied, "I'm in love with Tamar, my brother Absalom's sister." Jonadab said to him, "Lie down on your bed and pretend you're sick. When your father comes to see you, say to him, 'Please let my sister Tamar come and give me something to eat. Let her prepare food in my presence so I can watch and eat from her hand." (2 Samuel 13:1-5)

"He that walks with wise men shall be wise: but a companion of fools shall be destroyed." (Proverbs 13:20)

"Be not deceived: evil communications corrupt good manners." (I Corinthians 15:33)

"I made a covenant with mine eyes; why then should I think upon a maid? (Job 31:1)

"How shall we escape, if we neglect so great salvation; which at the first began to be spoken by the Lord, and was confirmed unto us by them that heard him?" (Hebrews 2:3)

"For the grace of God that brings salvation hath appeared to all men, teaching us that, denying ungodliness and worldly lusts, we should live soberly, righteously, and godly, in this present world;" (Titus 2:11-12)

There is none greater in this house than I; neither hath he kept back anything from me but thee, because thou art his wife: how then can I do this great wickedness, and sin against God?(Genesis 39:9)

"And be not conformed to this world: but be ye transformed by the renewing of your mind, that ye may prove what is that good, and acceptable, and perfect, will of God."(Romans 12:2)

"And even as they did not like to retain God in their knowledge, God gave them over to a reprobate mind, to do those things which are not convenient;" (Romans 1:28)

"Finally, brethren, whatsoever things are true, whatsoever things are honest, whatsoever things are just, whatsoever things are pure, whatsoever things are lovely, whatsoever things are of good report; if there be any virtue, and if there be any praise, think on these things."(Philippians 4:8)

"Flee fornication..."(1Corinthians 6:18)

"And it came to pass after these things, that his master's wife cast her eyes upon Joseph; and she said, lie with me. But he refused, and said unto his master's wife, Behold, my master knoweth not what is with me in the house, and he hath put all that he hath into my hand: he is not greater in this house than I; neither hath he kept back anything from me but thee, because thou art his wife: how then can I do this great wickedness, and sin against God? And it came to pass, as she spake to Joseph day by day, that he hearkened not unto her, to lie by her, or to be with her.

And it came to pass about this time that he went into the house to do his work; and there was none of the men of the house there within.

And she caught him by his garment, saying, lie with me: and he left his garment in her hand, and fled, and got him out."(Genesis 39: 7-12)

"For by means of a whorish woman a man is brought to a piece of bread: and the adulteress will hunt for the precious life. (Proverbs 6:26)

"Do not mix with winebibbers or with gluttonous eaters of meat; for the drunkard and the glutton will come to poverty, and drowsiness shall clothe a man with rags."(Proverbs 23:20-21)

CHAPTER 3

"And God said, Behold, I have given you every herb bearing seed, which is on the face of all the earth, and every tree, in the which is the fruit of a tree yielding seed; to you it shall be for meat....And God saw everything that he had made, and, behold, it was very good."(Genesis 1:29, 31)

"Be not among winebibbers; among riotous eaters of flesh: For the drunkard and the glutton shall come to poverty: and drowsiness shall clothe a man with rags... Who hath woe? Who hath sorrow? Who hath contentions? Who hath babbling? Who hath wounds without cause? Who hath redness of eyes? They that tarry long at the wine; they that go to seek mixed wine."(Proverbs 23:20-21, 29-30)

"And be not drunk with wine, wherein is excess..." (Ephesians 5:18)

"Drink no longer water, but use a little wine for thy stomach's sake and thine often infirmities."(I Timothy 5:23)

More dangerous than alcohol is the praise of people that gets people intoxicated(Acts 12:22-23).

"And take heed to yourselves, lest at any time your hearts be overcharged with surfeiting, and drunkenness, and cares of this life, and so that day come on you unawares." (Luke 21:34)

"Let us walk honestly, as in the day; not in rioting and drunkenness, not in chambering and wantonness, not in strife and envying". and to the Corinthian church, he wrote(Romans 13:13)

"But now I have written to you not to keep company, if any man that is called a brother be a fornicator, or covetous, or an idolater, or a reviler, or a drunkard, or an extortionist with such an one no not to eat". (1Corinthians 5:11)

"At the last it bites like a serpent, and stings like an adder. Your eyes shall behold strange women, and your heart shall utter perverse things. Yes, you shall be as he that lies down in the middle of the sea, or as he that lies on the top of a mast. They have stricken me, shall you say, and I was not sick; they have beaten me, and I felt it not: when shall I awake?

I will seek it yet again"(Proverbs 23:32-35)

"And the eyes of them both were opened, and they knew that they were naked; and they sewed fig leaves together, and made themselves aprons".

(Genesis 3:7)

"And Noah began to be a husbandman, and he planted a vineyard: And he drank of the wine, and was drunken; and he was uncovered within his tent". (Genesis 9:20-21)

*"Wine is a mocker, strong drink is raging: and whosoever is deceived thereby is not wise". (*Proverbs 20:1)

"Come, let us make our father drink wine, and we will lie with him, that we may preserve seed of our father.

And they made their father drink wine that night: and the firstborn went in, and lay with her father; and he perceived not when she lay down, nor when she arose. And it came to pass on the morrow, that the firstborn said unto the younger, Behold, I lay yester night with my father: let us make him drink wine this night also; and go thou in, and lie with him, that we may preserve seed of our father.... Thus were both the daughters of Lot with child by their father." (Genesis 19:32-36)

"For there is hope of a tree, if it be cut down, that it will sprout again, and that the tender branch thereof will not cease". (Job 14:7)

"Behold, I was shaped in iniquity; and in sin did my mother conceive me". (Psalm 51:5)

"And you shall know the truth, and the truth shall make you free". (John 8:32)

"That if you shall confess with your mouth the Lord Jesus, and shall believe in your heart that God has raised him from the dead, you shall be saved. For with the heart man believes to righteousness; and with the mouth confession is made to salvation". (Romans 10:9, 10)

"For if you live after the flesh, you shall die: but if you through the Spirit do mortify the deeds of the body, you shall live". Rom 8:13

"Abstain from all appearance of evil". (1Thessalonians 5:22)

CHAPTER 4

*"I find then a law, that, when I would do good, evil is present with me. But I see another law in my members, warring against the law of my mind, and bringing me into captivity to the law of sin which is in my members" (*Romans 7:21, 23)

"I will ascend above the heights of the clouds; I will be like the most High"

(Isaiah 14:14)

"Then went Samson to Gaza, and saw there an harlot, and went in unto her" (Judges 16:1)

"And it came to pass in an evening tide, that David arose from off his bed, and walked upon the roof of the king's house: and from the roof he saw a woman washing herself; and the woman was very beautiful to look upon"

(2Samuel 11:2)

... But because he was a thief, and had the bag, and bare what was put therein. (John 12:6)

"But Gehazi, the servant of Elisha the man of God, said, Behold, my master hath spared Naaman this Syrian, in not receiving at his hands that which he brought: but, as the LORD liveth, I will run after him, and take somewhat of him"(2Kings 5:20)

Now the sons of Eli were sons of Belial; they knew not the LORD. (1Samuel 2:12)

... Notwithstanding they hearkened not unto the voice of their father...

(1Samuel 2:25)

... And honorest thy sons above me, to make yourselves fat with the chiefest of all the offerings of Israel my people?(1Samuel 2:29)

"Train up a child in the way he should go: and when he is old, he will not depart from it" (Proverbs 22:6)

*"If thou doest well, shalt thou not be accepted? And if thou doest not well, sin lieth at the door. And unto thee shall be his desire, and thou shalt rule over him" (*Genesis 4:7)

"Blessed is the man that walketh not in the counsel of the ungodly, nor standeth in the way of sinners, nor sitteth in the seat of the scornful"

(Psalm 1:1)

"My son, if sinners entice thee, consent thou not. If they say, Come with us, let us lay wait for blood, let us lurk privily for the innocent without cause: My son, walk not thou in the way with them; refrain thy foot from their path"

(Proverbs 1:10-11, 15)

"... that I have set before you life and death, blessing and cursing: therefore choose life, that both thou and thy seed may live: (Deuteronomy 30:19)

"For by wise counsel thou shalt make thy war: and in multitude of counsellors there is safety"(Proverbs 24:6)

CHAPTER 5

"For this reason a man will leave his father and mother and be joined to his wife, and the two will become one flesh."(Matthew 19:5)

"So God created man in His own image; in the image of God He created him; male and female he created them" (Genesis 1:27)

"You shall not commit adultery."(Exodus 20:14)

"Thou shall love the LORD thy GOD with all your heart, and with all your soul, and with your entire mind" (Matthew 22:37)

"No one can serve two masters. Either you will hate one and love the other, or you will be devoted to one and despise the other" (Matthew 6:24)

"Do not deprive one another, except perhaps by agreement for a limited time, that you may devote yourselves to prayer; but then come together again, so that satan may not tempt you because of your lack of self-control." (1 Corinthians 7:5)

"But I say unto you, that whosoever looks on a woman to lust after her hath committed adultery with her already in his heart" (Matthew 5:28)

"Out of the heart of a man proceed evil thoughts, adulteries, fornications,"

(Mark 7:20-21)

"He who commits adultery lacks sense; he who does it destroys himself."

(Proverbs 6:32)

"For by means of a whorish woman a man is brought to a piece of bread"

(Proverbs 6:26)

"Stolen waters are sweet, and bread eaten in secret is pleasant"

(Proverbs 9:17)

"Behold, I will throw her onto a sick-bed, and those who commit adultery with her I will throw into great tribulation, unless they repent of their works."

(Revelation 2:22)

"Because she took her whoredom lightly, she polluted the land, committing adultery with stone and tree." (Jeremiah 3:9)

"They have eyes full of adultery, insatiable for sin. They entice unsteady souls. They have hearts trained in greed. Accursed children! (2Peter 2:14)

"When I fed them to the full, they committed adultery and trooped to the houses of whores." (Jeremiah 5:7)

CHAPTER 6

"For thy maker is thine husband, the lord of hosts is his name and their redeemer the Holy one of Israel; the God of the whole world shall he be called" (Isaiah 54:5)

"Therefore, let him that thinks he stands take heed lest he fall'.

(1 Corinthians 10:11)

"You shall not sow your vineyard with different kinds of seeds, lest the fruit of your seed which you have sown and the fruit of your vineyard be defiled"

(Deuteronomy 22:9)

"For the Word of God is living and powerful and sharper than any two-edged sword, piercing even to the dividing apart of soul and spirit, and of the joints and marrow, and is a discerner of the thoughts and intents of the heart" (Hebrew 4:12)

CHAPTER 7

Pride goes before a fall and a haughty spirit before destruction" (Proverb 16:18)

"..... A man can receive nothing, except it be given him from heaven"

(John 3:27)

"For I say, through the grace given unto me, to every man that is among you, not to think of himself more highly than he ought to think; but to think soberly, according as God has dealt to every man the measure of faith" (Romans 12:3)

"Thou was perfect in thy ways from the day that thou was created, till iniquity was found in thee" (Ezekiel 28:15)

*"These six things does the Lord hates, yes, seven are an abomination to Him: A proud look, a lying tongue, and hands that shed innocent blood. An heart that devises wicked imaginations, feet that be swift in running to mischief, A false witness that speaks lies, and he that sows discord among brothers" (*Proverbs 6:16-19)

"And upon a set day Herod, arrayed in royal apparel, sat upon his throne, and made an oration unto them. And the people gave a shout, saying, it is the voice of a god, and not of man. And immediately the angel of the Lord smote him, because he gave not God the glory and was eaten of worms and gave up the ghost" (Acts 12:21-23)

"... he said, this will I do, I will pull down my barns, and build Greater; and there will I bestow all my fruits and my goods. And I will say to my soul, Soul, you have much goods laid up for many years, take your ease, eat, drink, and be merry" (Luke 12:18, 19)

"... is not this great Babylon, that I have built for the kingdom by the might of my power, and for the honor of my majesty?" (Daniel 4:30)

"But when his heart was lifted up, and his mind hardened in pride, he was deposed from his kingly throne, and they took his glory from him... "And you his son, O Belshazzar, have not humbled your heart, though you knew all this" (Daniel 5:20.22)

"Every one that is proud in heart is an abomination to the Lord, through hand joined in hand, he shall not be unpunished" (Proverbs 16:5)

"When pride comes, then comes shame, but with the lowly is wisdom".

Proverbs 11:2

"In the mouth of the foolish is a rod of pride: but the lips of the wise shall preserve them" (Proverbs 14:3)

"Humble yourselves in the sight of the Lord, and He shall lift you up"

(James 4:10)

CHAPTER 8

"Be not hasty in thy spirit to be angry: for anger rests in the bosom of fools".

(Ecclesiastes 7:9)

"in your anger do not sin" do not let the sun goes down while you are still angry."

(Ephesians 4:26)

"Therefore the LORD was very angry with Israel, and removed them out of his sight: there was none left but the tribe of Judah only." **(2Kings 17:18)**

"An angry man stirs up dissension, and a hot-tempered one commits many sins" (Proverbs 29:22)

"But Naaman went away angry and said, I thought that he would surely come out to me and stand and call on the name of the Lord his God, wave his hand over the spot and cure me of my leprosy. 12 are not Abana and pharpar, the river in Damascus, better than any of the waters of Israel? Couldn't I washed in them and be cleansed? So, he turned and went off in a rage".

"If we confess our sins, he is faithful and just and will forgive us our sins and purify us from all unrighteous." (1 John 1:9)

"Be kind and compassionate to one and another, forgiving each other, just as in Christ God forgave" (Ephesians 4: 32)

"A gentle answer turns away wrath, but a harsh word stirs up anger." (Proverbs 15:1)

"in your anger do not sin" do not let the sun goes down while you are still angry."(Ephesians 4:26)

CHAPTER 9

" Looking diligently lest any man fall of the grace of God; lest any root of bitterness springing up trouble you, and lest any man thereby many be defiled."(Hebrews 12:15)

The Bible represents soil with the heart. *"The seeds that fell along the path stand for those who hear, but the Devil comes and takes the message away from their hearts in order to keep them from believing and being saved."*(Luke 8:12)

"Lest any root of bitterness springing up trouble you, and lest any man thereby many be defiled." (Hebrew 12:15)

"Now Israel loved Joseph more than all his children because he was the son of his old age and he made him a coat of many colors. And when his brethren saw that their father loved him more than all his brethren, they hated him, and could not speak peaceably unto him."(Genesis 37:3-4)

" when they saw him afar off, even before he came near unto them, they conspired against him to slay him and they said to one another, behold, this dreamer cometh" (Genesis 37:18 -19).

Repent therefore of this thy wickedness, and pray God, if perhaps the thought of thine heart may be forgiven thee, for I perceived that thou art in the gall of bitterness, and the bond of iniquity."(Acts 8:23)

" Give thanks in all circumstances; for this is the will of God in Christ Jesus for you." (1 Thessalonians 5:18).

"Looking diligently lest any man fails of the grace of God."(Hebrews 12:15)

"Come unto me, all ye that labor and are heavy laden, and I will give you rest." (Matthew 11:28)

"And be ye kind one to another, tenderhearted, forgiving one another, even as God for Christ's sake hath forgiven you."(Ephesians 4:32)

"And Joseph said unto his brethren, I am Joseph; doth my father yet live? And his brethren could not answer him; for they were troubled at his presence. And Joseph said unto his brethren, Come near to me, I pray you. And they came near. And he said, I am Joseph your brother, whom ye sold into Egypt. Now, therefore, be not grieved, nor angry with yourselves, that ye sold me hither: for God did send me before you to preserve life."

(Genesis 45:3-4)

"But as for you, ye thought evil against me; but God meant it unto good, to bring to pass, as it is this day, to save many people alive."(Genesis 50:20)

, *"...Father forgive them for they know not what they do"*(Luke 23:34)

"Keep thy heart with all diligence; for out of it are the issues of life."

(Proverbs 4:23)

CHAPTER 10

"For rebellion is as the sin of witchcraft, and stubbornness is as iniquity and idolatry. Because thou hast rejected the word of the LORD, he hath also rejected thee from being king." "For rebellion is as the sin of witchcraft."

(1 Samuel 15:23)

"How art thou fallen from heaven, O Lucifer, son of the morning? How art thou cut down to the ground, which didst weaken the nations! For thou hast said in thine heart, I will ascend into heaven; I will exalt my throne above the stars of God: I will also sit upon the mount of the congregation, in the sides of the north: I will ascend above the heights of the clouds; I will be like the most High."(Isaiah 14:12-14)

"Thus saith the LORD, Stand ye in the ways, and see, and ask for the old paths, where is the good way, and walk therein, and ye shall find rest for your souls. But they said we will not walk therein". (Jeremiah 6:16)

"Now go and smite Amalek, and utterly destroy all that they have, and spare them not; but slay both man and woman, infant and suckling, ox and sheep, camel and ass."(1 Samuel 15:3)

"And the LORD said unto Samuel, Hearken unto the voice of the people in all that they say unto thee: for they have not rejected thee, but they have rejected me, that I should not reign over them."(1 Samuel 8:7)

"...the locusts have no king, yet all of them march in rank;"(Proverbs 30:27)

"They shall run like mighty men; they shall climb the wall like men of war; and they shall march everyone on his ways, and they shall not break their ranks:" (Joel 2:7)

"Aaron shall be gathered unto his people: for he shall not enter into the land which I have given unto the children of Israel, because ye rebelled against my word at the water of Meribah,"(Numbers 20:24)

"Therefore thus saith the LORD; Behold, I will cast thee from off the face of the earth: this year thou shalt die because thou hast taught rebellion against the

LORD. So Hananiah the prophet died the same year in the seventh month" (Jeremiah 28:16 -17)

"Nevertheless they were disobedient, and rebelled against thee, and cast thy law behind their backs, and slew thy prophets who testified against them to turn them to thee, and they wrought great provocations. Therefore thou delivered them into the hand of their enemies, who vexed them: and in the time of their trouble, when they cried unto thee, thou heardest them from heaven; and according to thy manifold mercies thou gavest them saviors, who saved them out of the hand of their enemies." (Nehemiah 9: 26 -27)

"In whom the god of this world hath blinded the minds of them which believe not, lest the light of the glorious gospel of Christ, who is the image of God, should shine unto them." (2 Corinthians 4: 4)

"If my people, which are called by my name, shall humble themselves, and pray, and seek my face, and turn from their wicked ways; then will I hear from heaven, and will forgive their sin, and will heal their land." (2 Chronicles 7:14)

"And unto one, he gave five talents, to another two, and to another one; to every man according to his several abilities; and straightway took his journey." (Matthew 25:15)

"Humble yourselves in the sight of the Lord, and he shall lift you up." (James 4:10)

"Oh that men would praise the LORD for his goodness, and for his wonderful works to the children of men." (Psalms 107:8)

CHAPTER 11

"For you are still carnal. For where there are envy, strife and divisions among you, are you not carnal and behaving like mere men?"

(1 Corinthians 3:3)

"Behold, how good and how pleasant it is for brethren to dwell together in unity!" (Psalms 133:1)

"Only by PRIDE comes contention: but with the well advised there is wisdom." (Proverbs 13:10)

"He that is of a proud heart stirreth up strife..." (Proverbs 28:25)

"A wrathful man stirred up strife: but he that is low to anger appeased strife." (Proverbs 15:18)

Despite the fact that Saul was the anointed King of Israel, he had God's Spirit and favor upon on him yet; he became jealous of David's ability, success, and popularity among God's people. Instead of celebrating this huge success at this time, Saul allowed jealousy to grow in his heart. This led to disobedience and other sinful acts. (1 Samuel 18: 6 – 9)

The Bible says. "For wherever there are jealousy and selfish ambition, there you will find disorder and evil of every kind." (James 3:16)

"Hatred stirreth up strife: but love covereth all sins." (Proverbs 10:12)

A soft answer turneth away wrath: but grievous words stir up anger." (Proverbs 15:1)

"Where no wood is, there the fire goeth out: so where there is no talebearer, the strife ceaseth." (Proverbs 26:20)

"From whence come wars and fightings among you? come they not hence, even of your lusts that war in your members? " (James 4:1)

"It is better to dwell in the corner of the housetop, than with a brawling woman in a wide house." (Proverbs 21:19)

"Envying, murders, drunkenness, revellings, and such like: of which I tell you before, as I have also told you in time past, that they which do such things shall not inherit the kingdom of God." (Galatians 5:21)

"... The land was not able to bear them, that they might dwell together: for their substance was great, so that they could not dwell together. And there was a strife between the herdsmen of Abram's cattle and the herd men of Lot's cattle: and the Canaanite and the Perizzite dwelled then in the land.

(Genesis 13: 6-7)

"Let there be no strife between you and me, and between your herdsmen and my herdsmen, for we are kinsmen" (Genesis 13:8).

"Pleasant words are a honeycomb, sweet to the soul and healing to the bones." (Proverbs 16:24)

"Let nothing be done through strife or vainglory, but in lowliness of mind let each esteem other better than themselves." (Philippians 2:3)

"Follow peace with all men, and holiness, without which no man shall see the Lord." (Proverbs 12:14)

CHAPTER 12

"If you want people to like you, forgive them when they wrong you. Remembering wrongs can break up a friendship." (Proverbs 17:9)

"And be ye kind one to another, tenderhearted, forgiving one another, even as God for Christ's sake hath forgiven you."(Ephesians 4:32)

"No," she answered. "To send me away like this is a greater crime than what you just did!" But Ammon would not listen to her; he called in his personal servant and said, "Get this woman out of my sight!

(2 Samuel 13:14-17)

"The servant fell on his knees before the king. 'Be patient with me,' he begged, and I will pay you everything!"(Mathew 18:26)

"So if you are about to offer your gift to God at the altar and there you remember that your brother has something against you, leave your gift there in front of the altar, go at once and make peace with your brother, and then come back and offer your gift to God."(Matthew 5:23-24)

"If your BROTHER sins against you go to him and SHOW HIM HIS FAULT..." (Matthew 18:15)

"And Absalom hated Amnon so much for having raped his sister Tamar that he would no longer even SPEAK TO HIM."(2 Samuel 13:22)

"Then Peter came to Jesus and asked, "Lord, if my brother keeps on sinning against me, how many times do I have to forgive him? Seven times?"(Matthew 18:21)

"Wherewithal shall a young man cleanse his way? By taking heed there to according to thy word."(Psalms 119:9)

"Is any among you afflicted? Let him pray. Is any merry? let him sing psalms." (James 5:13)

"For if ye forgive men their trespasses, your heavenly Father will also forgive you: But if ye forgive not men their trespasses, neither will your Father forgive your trespasses."(Matthew 6:14)

END NOTES

INTRODUCTION

1. Deuteronomy 22:9 Do Not Plant Your Vineyard with Two Types ... (n.d.). Retrieved from https://biblehub.com/deuteronomy/22-9.htm
2. Bible Study | The Agape geek Blog | Page 8. (n.d.). Retrieved from https://agapegeek.com/category/bible-study/page/8/
3. John 3:6 KJV "that Which Is Born Of The Flesh Is Flesh ... (n.d.). Retrieved from https://www.kingjamesbibleonline.org/John-3-6/
4. Galatians 5:21 KJV "envying, Murders, Drunkenness ... (n.d.). Retrieved from https://www.kingjamesbibleonline.org/Galatians-5-21/
5. Deuteronomy Chapter 22 KJV - King James Version. (n.d.). Retrieved from https://www.kingjamesbibleonline.org/Deuteronomy-Chapter-22/
6. Daniel 5:20 KJV "but When His Heart Was Lifted Up, And His ... (n.d.). Retrieved from https://www.kingjamesbibleonline.org/Daniel-5-20/
7. Ecclesiastes 7:9 KJV: Be Not Hasty In Thy Spirit To Be ... (n.d.). Retrieved from https://biblehub.com/KJV/ecclesiastes/7-9.htm

CHAPTER ONE

1. Isaiah 2:8 KJV - Their Land Also Is Full Of Idols; They ... (n.d.). Retrieved from https://www.biblegateway.com/passage/?search=Isaiah+2:8&version=KJV
2. James 4:1 What Causes Conflicts And Quarrels Among You ... (n.d.). Retrieved from https://www.biblehub.com/james/4-1.htm

3. Matthew 13:4-8 KJV - And When He Sowed, Some Seeds Fell By ... (n.d.). Retrieved fromhttps://www.biblegateway.com/passage/?search=Matthew+13%3A4-8&version=KJV
4. How Our Emotions Affect Our Heart Health | Edward-Elmhurst ... (n.d.). Retrieved from https://www.eehealth.org/blog/2019/03/emotions-heart-health/
5. Colossians 3:5-10 ESV - Put To Death Therefore What Is ... (n.d.). Retrieved from https://www.biblegateway.com/passage/?search=Colossians+3%3A5-10&version=ESV
6. Hebrews 13:5 KJV "[let Your] Conversation [be] Without ... (n.d.). Retrieved from https://www.kingjamesbibleonline.org/Hebrews-13-5/
7. 1 Corinthians 5:11 But Now I Am Writing You Not To ... (n.d.). Retrieved from https://biblehub.com/1—corinthians/5-11.htm
8. The word covetousness in the Hebrew word is translated as the word "*betsa*," which means 'to plunder', 'to acquire' or 'possess an insatiable desire for honest gain' (Exodus 18:21)
9. Joshua 7:21 KJV "when I Saw Among The Spoils A Goodly ... (n.d.). Retrieved from https://www.kingjamesbibleonline.org/Joshua-7-21/
10. John 12:6 KJV "this He Said, Not That He Cared For The ... (n.d.). Retrieved from https://www.kingjamesbibleonline.org/John-12-6/
11. Jeremiah 5:7 ESV: "how Can I Pardon You? Your Children ... (n.d.). Retrieved from https://biblehub.com/esv/Jeremiah/5-7.htm

CHAPTER TWO

1. Genesis 39:9 KJV "[there Is] None Greater In This House ... (n.d.). Retrieved from https://www.kingjamesbibleonline.org/Genesis-39-9/
2. The word *Koinonia* in the Greek language means intimacy.
3. Merriam-Webster dictionary defines fornication as a consensual sexual intercourse between two persons (male and female) not married to each other.
4. Hebrews 13:5 KJV "[let Your] Conversation [be] Without ... (n.d.). Retrieved from https://www.kingjamesbibleonline.org/Hebrews-13-5/
5. Joshua 7:21 KJV "when I Saw Among The Spoils A Goodly ... (n.d.). Retrieved from https://www.kingjamesbibleonline.org/Joshua-7-21/
6. John 12:6 KJV "this He Said, Not That He Cared For The ... (n.d.). Retrieved from https://www.kingjamesbibleonline.org/John-12-6/

7. 2 Samuel 13:1-20 - CSB Bible - Some Time Passed. David's ... (n.d.). Retrieved from https://www.biblestudytools.com/csb/2-samuel/passage/?q=2-samuel+13:1-20
8. Proverbs 4:23 Guard Your Heart With All Diligence, For ... (n.d.). Retrieved from https://biblehub.com/proverbs/4-23.htm
9. 2 Samuel 13:1-20 - CSB Bible - Some Time Passed. David's ... (n.d.). Retrieved from https://www.biblestudytools.com/csb/2-samuel/passage/?q=2-samuel+13:1-20
10. Proverbs 13:20 He Who Walks With The Wise Will Become Wise ... (n.d.). Retrieved from https://www.biblehub.com/proverbs/13-20.htm
11. Full Text Of "the Works Of Charles Haddon Spurgeon". (n.d.). Retrieved from https://archive.org/stream/MorningAndEveningDailyReadings/Charles%20Haddon%20Spu
12. Genesis 39:9 KJV "[there Is] None Greater In This House ... (n.d.). Retrieved from https://www.kingjamesbibleonline.org/Genesis-39-9/

CHAPTER THREE

1. Proverbs 23:30 KJV: They That Tarry Long At The Wine; They ... (n.d.). Retrieved from https://biblehub.com/KJV/proverbs/23-30.htm
2. Romans 8:13 For If You Live According To The Flesh, You ... (n.d.). Retrieved from https://www.biblehub.com/romans/8-13.htm
3. Luke Chapter 21 KJV - King James Version. (n.d.). Retrieved from https://www.kingjamesbibleonline.org/Luke-Chapter-21/
4. Philippians 4:8 Finally, Brothers, Whatever Is True ... (n.d.). Retrieved from https://biblehub.com/philippians/4-8.htm
5. 1 Corinthians 5:11 KJV "but Now I Have Written Unto You ... (n.d.). Retrieved from https://www.kingjamesbibleonline.org/1-Corinthians-5-11/
6. The Word Net dictionary describes a drunken person as one who is "made sottish, senseless, or infatuated by alcohol or wine.
7. Proverbs 23:34 You Will Be Like One Sleeping On The High ... (n.d.). Retrieved from https://biblehub.com/proverbs/23-34.htm
8. Genesis 3:7 And The Eyes Of Both Of Them Were Opened, And ... (n.d.). Retrieved from https://www.biblehub.com/genesis/3-7.htm
9. Psalm 51:5 Surely I Was Brought Forth In Iniquity; I Was ... (n.d.). Retrieved from https://biblehub.com/psalms/51-5.htm
10. Life Inspired By God: Living Life In, With, And On Purpose ... (n.d.). Retrieved from https://lifeinspiredbygod.blogspot.com/2009/

CHAPTER FOUR

1. Immoral | Definition of Immoral by Merriam-Webster. (n.d.). Retrieved from https://www.merriam-webster.com/dictionary/immoral
2. Romans 7:23 KJV "but I See another Law In My Members ... (n.d.). Retrieved from https://www.kingjamesbibleonline.org/Romans-7-23/
3. Merriam-Webster dictionary describes immorality as unlawful, unethical, sinful, evil among others. Not morally good or right, morally evil or wrong.
4. Isaiah 14:12 KJV "how Art Thou Fallen From Heaven, O ... (n.d.). Retrieved from https://www.kingjamesbibleonline.org/Isaiah-14-12/
5. 2 Kings Chapter 5 KJV - King James Version. (n.d.). Retrieved from https://www.kingjamesbibleonline.org/2-Kings-Chapter-5/
6. 1 Samuel 2:25 KJV "if One Man Sin Against Another, The ... (n.d.). Retrieved from https://www.kingjamesbibleonline.org/1-Samuel-2-25/
7. Hebrews 11 Commentary - A.W. Pink's Commentary on John And ... (n.d.). Retrieved from https://odl.studylight.org/commentaries/awp/hebrews-11.html
8. Genesis 4:7 KJV "if Thou Doest Well, Shalt Thou Not Be ... (n.d.). Retrieved from https://www.kingjamesbibleonline.org/Genesis-4-7/

CHAPTER FIVE

1. Ephesians 5:31 "for This Reason A Man Will Leave His ... (n.d.). Retrieved from https://biblehub.com/ephesians/5-31.htm
2. 5 Types Of Adultery You Probably Didn't Know About L Facts ... (n.d.). Retrieved from https://www.beliefnet.com/love-family/relationships/affairs-and-divorce/5-types
3. 1 Corinthians 7:5 Do Not Deprive One Another, Except By ... (n.d.). Retrieved from https://biblehub.com/1—corinthians/7-5.htm
4. 40 Consequences of Adultery | Family life®. (n.d.). Retrieved from https://www.familylife.com/articles/topics/marriage/troubled-marriage/infidelity
5. Marital Infidelity Healing - Maritalhealing.com. (n.d.). Retrieved from https://maritalhealing.com/conflicts/maritalinfidelity.php
6. 2 Peter 2:14 Their Eyes Are Full Of Adultery; Their Desire ... (n.d.). Retrieved from https://biblehub.com/2—peter/2-14.htm

CHAPTER SIX

1. Thy Maker Is Thine Husband - Growing In His Grace. (n.d.). Retrieved from https://www.growinginhisgrace.com/thy-maker-is-thine-husband/
2. A Jealous God - Allaboutgod.com. (n.d.). Retrieved from https://www.allaboutgod.com/a-jealous-god.htm
3. Deuteronomy 22:9 Do Not Plant Your Vineyard With Two Types ... (n.d.). Retrieved from https://biblehub.com/deuteronomy/22-9.htm

CHAPTER SEVEN

1. Pride And Humility – Lucretia Cargill. (n.d.). Retrieved from https://lucretiashaw.wordpress.com/2018/01/03/pride-and-humility/
2. John 3:27 John Replied, "a Man Can Receive Only What Is ... (n.d.). Retrieved from https://biblehub.com/john/3-27.htm
3. Proverbs 8:13 - Bible Gateway. (n.d.). Retrieved from https://www.biblegateway.com/verse/en/Proverbs%208%3A13
4. Bible Gateway Passage: Acts 12:22-24 - King James Version. (n.d.). Retrieved from https://www.biblegateway.com/passage/?search=Acts+12:22-24&version=KJV
5. Bible Gateway Passage: Acts 12:22-24 - King James Version. (n.d.). Retrieved from https://www.biblegateway.com/passage/?search=Acts+12:22-24&version=KJV
6. Full Text Of "the Works Of Charles Haddon Spurgeon". (n.d.). Retrieved from https://archive.org/stream/MorningAndEveningDailyReadings/Charles%20Haddon%20Spu
7. Daniel 5:20 KJV "but When His Heart Was Lifted Up, And His ... (n.d.). Retrieved from https://www.kingjamesbibleonline.org/Daniel-5-20/

CHAPTER EIGHT

1. Ecclesiastes 7:9 KJV: Be Not Hasty In Thy Spirit To Be ... (n.d.). Retrieved from https://biblehub.com/KJV/ecclesiastes/7-9.htm
2. The word anger in the Greek language is "orgizo" which means to make annoyed, provoke to rage or to irritate.
3. 2 Kings 17:18 KJV "therefore The Lord Was Very Angry With ... (n.d.). Retrieved from https://www.kingjamesbibleonline.org/2-Kings-17-18/
4. 1 Samuel 18:7 And As The Women Danced, They Sang Out ... (n.d.). Retrieved from https://www.biblehub.com/1—samuel/18-7.htm
5. 2 Kings 5 NIV - Naaman Healed Of Leprosy - Now Naaman ... (n.d.). Retrieved from https://www.biblegateway.com/passage/?search=2%20Kings%205&version=NIV
6. Genesis 34:31 But Simeon And Levi Answered, "should He ... (n.d.). Retrieved from https://biblehub.com/genesis/34-31.htm
7. Proverbs 15:1 A Gentle Answer Turns Away Wrath, But A ... (n.d.). Retrieved from https://biblehub.com/proverbs/15-1.htm
8. Ephesians 4:26 - "in Your Anger Do Not Sin": Do Not ... (n.d.). Retrieved from https://www.biblegateway.com/passage/?search=Ephesians%204:26

CHAPTER NINE

1. Five Key Differences Between Anger And Bitterness. (n.d.). Retrieved from https://thegrassgetsgreener.com/anger-and-bitterness/
2. The word "Bitterness" comes from the Greek language, "Pikria," which means acridity, harshness, unhappiness, and irascibility.
3. Understanding The Difference Between Anger And Bitterness. (n.d.). Retrieved from https://mindbodynetwork.com/article/understanding-the-difference-between-anger-a
4. Luke 8, Good News Translation (GNT) | The Bible App. (n.d.). Retrieved from https://www.bible.com/bible/68/LUK.8.GNT
5. The Root Of Bitterness - What It Is & How To Get Rid Of It. (n.d.). Retrieved fromhttps://www.crosswalk.com/faith/spiritual-life/the-root-of-bitterness-1167870.ht
6. Sunday Sermon: 'joseph – Bitterness Or Betterness ... (n.d.). Retrieved from https://pastorterryblog.wordpress.com/2011/07/03/sunday-sermon-joseph-bitterness
7. Beware Of Bitterness Ephesians 4:30-32. (n.d.). Retrieved from http://www.brandonweb.com/sermons/sermonpages/ephesians18.htm
8. Romans 8:28 And We Know That God Works All Things Together ... (n.d.). Retrieved from https://biblehub.com/romans/8-28.htm

9. Genesis 45:3 KJV "and Joseph Said Unto His Brethren, I [am ... (n.d.). Retrieved from https://www.kingjamesbibleonline.org/Genesis-45-3/
10. The Root Of Bitterness Sermon By Rodelio Mallari, Hebrews ... (n.d.). Retrieved from https://www.sermoncentral.com/sermons/the-root-of-bitterness-rodelio-mallari-ser

CHAPTER TEN

1. Isaiah 14:12 KJV "how Art Thou Fallen From Heaven, O ... (n.d.). Retrieved from https://www.kingjamesbibleonline.org/Isaiah-14-12/
2. The Hebrew word "qecem," means "Witchcraft or divination."
3. Jeremiah 6:16 KJV "thus Saith The Lord, Stand Ye In The ... (n.d.). Retrieved from https://www.kingjamesbibleonline.org/Jeremiah-6-16/
4. A.W. Tozer Quotes (Author of the Pursuit of God) (page 4 ... (n.d.). Retrieved from https://www.goodreads.com/author/quotes/1082290.A—W—Tozer?page=4
5. 1 Samuel 8:7-9 KJV - And The Lord Said Unto Samuel ... (n.d.). Retrieved from https://www.biblegateway.com/passage/?search=1+Samuel+8%3A7-9&version=KJV
6. Numbers 20:24 KJV "Aaron Shall Be Gathered Unto His People ... (n.d.). Retrieved from https://www.kingjamesbibleonline.org/Numbers-20-24/
7. Jeremiah 28:16 Therefore, This Is What the Lord Says: 'I ... (n.d.). Retrieved from https://biblehub.com/Jeremiah/28-16.htm
8. Nehemiah 9:26 KJV "nevertheless They Were Disobedient, And ... (n.d.). Retrieved from https://www.kingjamesbibleonline.org/Nehemiah-9-26/
9. 2 Chronicles 7:14 KJV - If My People, Which Are Called By ... (n.d.). Retrieved from https://www.biblegateway.com/passage/?search=2%20Chronicles+7:14&version=KJV
10. Psalms 107:8 KJV "oh That [men] Would Praise The Lord [for ... (n.d.). Retrieved from https://www.kingjamesbibleonline.org/Psalms-107-8/

CHAPTER ELEVEN

1. 1 Corinthians 3:3 KJV "for Ye Are Yet Carnal: For Whereas ... (n.d.). Retrieved from https://www.kingjamesbibleonline.org/1-Corinthians-3-3/

2. The word strife is coined out from Hebrew language **"Madon"** and Greek **"Eris"** which means a contest, quarrel, uncertain affinity, contention, bitter disagreement, conflict.
3. Proverbs 15:1 A Gentle Answer Turns Away Wrath, But A ... (n.d.). Retrieved from https://biblehub.com/proverbs/15-1.htm
4. 1 Samuel 18:6-16 KJV - And It Came To Pass As They Came ... (n.d.). Retrieved from https://www.biblegateway.com/passage/?search=1+samuel+18%3A6-16&version=KJV
5. Proverbs 15:1 A Gentle Answer Turns Away Wrath, But A ... (n.d.). Retrieved from https://biblehub.com/proverbs/15-1.htm
6. Galatians 5:21 KJV "envying, Murders, Drunkenness ... (n.d.). Retrieved from https://www.kingjamesbibleonline.org/Galatians-5-21/
7. Things That Can Kill Christians: Strife Is A Killer. (n.d.). Retrieved from http://www.biblecities.com/strife.htm
8. Pike, S. (2018). He who guards his tongue keeps himself from calamity. Claresholm Local Press, p. A.16.

CHAPTER TWELVE

1. Proverbs 17:9 GNT - Bible Gateway. (n.d.). Retrieved from https://www.biblegateway.com/passage/?search=Proverbs+17%3A9&version=GNT
2. 2 Samuel 13:16 "no," She Replied, "sending Me Away Is ... (n.d.). Retrieved from https://biblehub.com/2—samuel/13-16.htm
3. 1 Kings 2:6 - GNT - You Know What To Do; You Must Not Let... (n.d.). Retrieved from https://www.studylight.org/bible/GNT/1-kings/2-6.html
4. 1 Kings 2:1-25 When David Was About To Die, He Called His ... (n.d.). Retrieved from https://www.bible.com/bible/296/1KI.2.1-25.GNB
5. Matthew 18:26 Then The Servant Fell On His Knees Before ... (n.d.). Retrieved from https://www.biblehub.com/matthew/18-26.htm
6. Matthew 18:21 Then Peter Came To Jesus And Asked, "lord ... (n.d.). Retrieved from https://biblehub.com/matthew/18-16.htm
7. Psalm 119:9 How Can A Young Man Keep His Way Pure? By ... (n.d.). Retrieved from https://biblehub.com/psalms/119-9.htm

APPENDIX A

GLOSSARY OF TERMS AND DEFINITIONS

Addiction: Repeated involvement with a substance or activity despite substantial harm it causes.

Adultery: Extramarital sex that willfully and maliciously interferes with marriage relations

Bacchus: god of wine

Consequences: The outcome of an event

Conspiracy: A secret agreement between two or more people to perform an unlawful act

Defilement: The state of being polluted

Drunkenness: Being intoxicated by alcohol

Fornication: Sexual intercourse between people not married to each other

Idolatry: Worship of something or someone other than God.

Immorality: Behavior that is morally wrong

Lust: A strong feeling of wanting something

Nazarite: A person set aside for the service of God with a vow to avoid drinking wine, cutting the hair among others.

Rebellion: Opposition to one in authority or dominance

Seed: A small round or oval object produced by a plant and from which, when it is planted, a new one can grow.

APPENDIX B-
WORLD STATISTICS ON ADULTERY

The top 10 countries in the world that accept infidelity

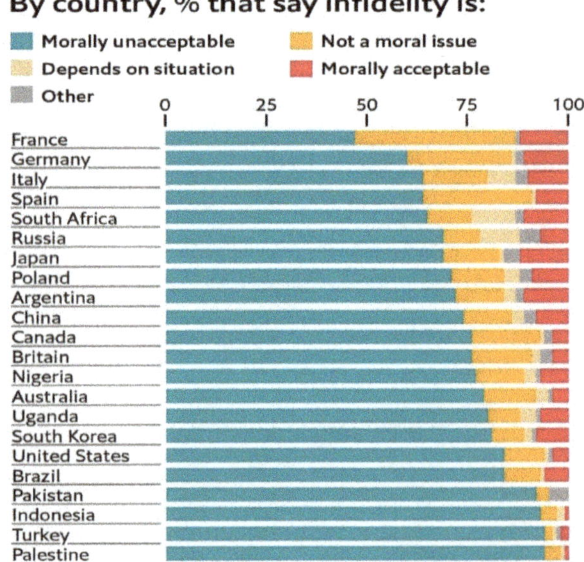

Source:https://www.1843magazine.com/data-graphic/what-the-numbers-say/infidelity-around-the-world

Affairs considered not to be a moral issue (top 10)

1. France (40%)
2. Spain (27%)
3. Germany (26%)
4. Senegal (24%)
5. Canada (17%)
6. Chile (16%)
7. Italy (16%)
8. Britain (15%)
9. Japan (14%)
10. Australia (13%)

Source:https://www.first4lawyers.com/news-and-resources/the-top-10-countries-in-the-world-that-accept-infidelity/

ABOUT THE AUTHOR

Born March 3, 1959 in Louisville, Kentucky, Dr. Theodore L. Dones is an apostolic revivalist. He is the president and founder of Messengers of Fire Ministries. His ministry itinerates across the nation and crosses over denominational boundaries and geographical borders to fulfill what the Lord has called him to do: to stir up the churches, telling them to get ready for the coming revival.

Dr. Dones' greatest desire is this one thing: To be an instrument for God to, "open the eyes of His people and turn them from darkness to light, from the power of satan to God so that they may receive forgiveness of sins and inheritance among those who are sanctified by faith in Christ." He has worked vigilantly, using every resource and opportunity that God sends his way to accomplish his call.

Apostle Ted Dones attended International Circle of Faith College, Seminaries and Universities, joining alumni such as Pastor Paula White, Bishop Noel Jones, attorney Julian McPhillips, Bishop Paul Morton and other distinguished men and women. He lays down his life to help leadership grow in foundational truths that must be established before works of faith are built upon them. He has helped thousands tear down the unproductive ways which seem right to a man and replaced them with the ways of the Lord.

Ultimately, Dr. Dones has seen his vision fulfilled which the Lord gave him several years ago. He will build a 2500-seat training center with an emphasis on the nine Gifts of the Spirit. This center will act as a resource hub for the Five Fold Ministry and believers will be dispersed out into the world, fully equipped to make disciples. The fruit of his international ministry has been in the works for more than fifteen years. Five Fold Connection (www.fivefoldconnection.com) is a leadership networking site equivalent to Facebook, which he has recently launched and is connecting God's people with rapid results. This site provides a God-rated environment for families to enjoy Godly conversations, posts, and teachings. Christian gaming and other enhancements are being added as well.

The Messengers of Fire Bible College, which opened in 2011, affords everyone an opportunity to learn God's Word online: www.mofmchristianuniversity.org. Dr. Ted Dones has reached nations for God on television (WBNA TV Channel 285) and radio, affecting many souls during his recent trip to Africa. Leadership conferences, weekly local church services and international ministry are just another part of Dr. Dones 'everyday life. He relies fully on God's grace, presence and anointing, being fully aware of his personal inability to do anything good without Christ. He watches in amazement as God continually sends people into his life to support all aspects of the vision. He greatly anticipates the day when God's plan is complete and all the glory is given to God the Father! Dr. Dones is married to Janet; they have been married since 1980 and have one daughter and four grandchildren.

www.ingramcontent.com/pod-product-compliance
Lightning Source LLC
Chambersburg PA
CBHW071853090426
42811CB00004B/593

* 9 7 8 0 5 7 8 5 6 9 4 9 9 *